TEXAS A&M UNIVERSITY PRESS   COLLEGE STATION

Adventures
in Texas Gardening

NUMBER 49
Louise Lindsey Merrick Natural Environment Series

Adventures
in Texas Gardening

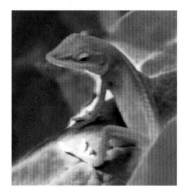

BILL SCHEICK

Library of Congress Cataloging-in-Publication Data

Names: Scheick, William J., author.
Title: Adventures in Texas gardening / Bill Scheick.
Other titles: Louise Lindsey Merrick natural environment series; no. 49.
Description: First edition. | College Station: Texas A&M University Press,
[2017] | Series: Louise Lindsey Merrick natural environment series;
number 49 | Includes bibliographical references and index.
Identifiers: LCCN 2016049044 (print) | LCCN 2016051148 (ebook) |
ISBN 9781623495176 (flex with flaps: alk. paper) | ISBN 9781623495183 (ebook)
Subjects: LCSH: Gardening—Texas.
Classification: LCC SB453.2.T4 S34 2017 (print) | LCC SB453.2.T4 (ebook) |
DDC 635.09764—dc23
LC record available at https://lccn.loc.gov/2016049044

For Catherine
who played with me in the dirt

&

for Chris Corby
who encouraged me to harvest words from that dirt

Contents

Adventures
in Texas Gardening

Introduction

I know what I am supposed to say here. An introduction to a proper gardening book should promise that it is the last guide any gardener will ever need. It should promise to be a definitive step-by-step, how-to handbook with fail/foolproof recommendations. Oh, and it should pledge to satisfy every gardener's quest for the four E's: Easiness, Effectiveness, Efficiency, and Economy.

That's how to sell a book, but these four E's are a far cry from my experience of the challenging realities of gardening in Texas. Those daunting realities can't even be summarized finally in any simple list. Nor would such a list be worth the bother in a region where the total of the four E's that Texas gardeners can truthfully count on is E^4—Effort, four times itself.

Mine, then, is not a proper gardening book. It's designed as a conversational, yet hopefully helpful, account of how things went for me and for some other Texan gardening addicts I met over the years. It's about big gardening efforts, such as transforming an entire backyard, dealing with dogs in the home landscape, coping with foraging wildlife, stumbling into pond-keeping, decontaminating a droughty veggie patch, and giving up on lawns. It's about growing an in-ground Christmas tree at home, calculating the age of a cedar elm, sculpting plants to look like little trees, raising houseplants outdoors as landscape additions, planning for winter berries, fostering vanishing bees, rethinking premature herb-flowering, pondering the why of odd black and green flowers, enjoying the night garden after speculating about the moon's influence on what we grow. It's about ten Texans' fascination—sometimes obsession—with prickly pears, salvias, cupheas, mini-callas, daylilies, irises, buckwheat, orchids, and African violets.

I have lived and gardened in Central Texas since 1969. I've gardened at three different addresses there and also at a home in the

Persian lilac (Syringa × persica)

Hill Country. What worked at one location did not necessarily work at another, even when only a few miles apart. Surprisingly, tried-and-true Texas-resilient cultivars, such as the Knock-Out rose series, behaved differently at these places. Sometimes the most basic gardening successes at one home simply could not be duplicated with ease at another. In fact, each yard presented different difficulties that ultimately required trial-and-error approaches.

There were, I admit, stretches of pure stubbornness on my part that could only end badly. That was the case with a Persian lilac (*Syringa × persica*), known for better heat tolerance than most other lilacs but still stressed by the heat zone (not the cold-hardiness zone) of the Austin area. It did not help that the cold-hardiness zones for Texas eventually became officially hotter, according to the United States Department of Agriculture. I have always loved the scent and beauty of lilacs, which during my New Jersey childhood gloriously signaled the joys of spring and (equally gloriously) forecasted the approaching end of the always-dreaded school year.

Decades later, a former university student of mine in Cedar Park had managed to keep her nearly two-foot, in-ground Persian lilac alive, and one spring she even saw a few blooms, which she proudly showed me. Mine, despite being thoroughly pampered in Oak Hill (in southwestern Travis County), stayed well under two feet for most of its life. After thirteen years, my Persian lilac had eventually grown to four feet, but was sparse and wispy—a Charlie Brown Christmas-tree sort of plant. It had twice (during March in both years) produced a few small panicles of fragrant blooms, which I greedily sniffed at as gleefully as a dog. Then during a following year of record-setting drought and heat, the lilac suddenly died. My defiant trial-and-error experiment in zone-pushing that poor lilac was over.

I admit to a trial-and-error gardening attitude with some discomfort. I had acquired plenty of botanic and horticultural learning before and since the long-ago day when I graduated college with my teacher-certification in high-school biology. The courses taught by my botany professor (who turned out to be my favorite college instructor) were demanding—each lecture packed, each exam rigorous, and each lab practicum bruising. Surely, one might imagine, I must have learned a thing or two.

Since then, much has changed in the biological sciences, which would shift dramatically from morphology to biochemistry and genomes. We'll note later in this book, for instance, how flowers long thought to be asters on the basis of their appearance (their morphological features) proved genetically to be their own unique group. They still look like asters and we still call them asters, but they aren't asters.

Nature remains very complicated and mysterious.

Actually, even when I was an undergraduate, there were inklings of vexing unsettledness in biology. Some biological understandings that seemed to be obvious enough were not quite so simple. Trouble could flicker like faint lightening just over the horizon of biology-textbook certainties. For instance, the division of life into only two kingdoms (plant and animal) seemed evident, but that concept failed to neatly contain everything we studied in class.

That was true for slime molds, which were classification outliers when I was an undergraduate student and remain considerably more puzzling today. Carnivorous plants likewise did not quite fit into the two-kingdom scheme. Since carnivorous plants produce chloroplasts, they photosynthesize like other flora. But they tend to grow in nutrient-poor habitats and so require supplemental minerals, particularly nitrogen and phosphorus. In order to meet their nutritional needs, carnivorous plants mimic animal behavior by capturing and digesting insects. Their predatory strategies are multiple, cunning, and stunningly strange. We still do not understand much about these nerveless and muscleless plants, which are nonetheless somehow capable of preying on critters that do possess ganglions and striated muscles. The mystery has only deepened recently with the discovery that the genome of the Venus flytrap seems to partially replicate the nerve-DNA of the very insects it devours. The Venus flytrap is what it eats!

I remember also being fascinated in college by the enigma of euglenas, single-cell organisms that refused to belong to just the plant or the animal kingdom. Euglenas were flagellate and so exhibited the mobility of animals. Yet most could feed themselves by means of their photosynthesizing chloroplasts. Today these organisms are thought to be neither animals nor plants, which is one way to skirt the older basic puzzle about them. Obviously, euglenas are still causing trouble. Debate is ongoing about whether they belong to the Protista kingdom, which is a new hypothetical biological division. Blame the electron microscope and other technological advances, which have revealed and released the mischievous devil that always lurks in the details—in this instance, the devilry previously unacknowledged in our earlier belief in only two kingdoms.

At present it remains open to debate as to how many kingdoms define terrestrial life. There has likewise been an attempt to shift the discussion away from kingdoms to domains, including one that unites animals and fungi. That may seem a bit fantastical, but continuing scientific research often erodes the established boundaries of widely held understandings. So far, biology has not been able to settle on firm, fixed categories for life. At present, one such ongoing boundary-erosion compromises our standard perception of the dissimilarity between plants and animals. Researchers are now finding that genetic differences between plants and animals are not as distinct as we have tended to believe.

All of this is intrinsically interesting, but my point finally is that I try to keep up with new findings in botanic knowledge. I also have a room full of previously read and consulted gardening books, not only

Venus flytrap

really good ones but also works I have publicly reviewed during the last decade or so. Then there are my nearly 200 gardening articles published statewide in newspapers and magazines. Surely, a scientifically grounded, proficient approach must have prevailed throughout my gardening life, right?

It is true that all that learned knowledge did and still does help me—somewhat. Yet the simple humiliating fact remains, as we all know, that "The best laid schemes of mice and men / Often go awry." Nature trumps book learning. And nature in Texas is . . . well, maybe the best way to sum up nature in this large, environmentally diverse state might be to repeat a popular Lone Star saying adapted from a comment by General Philip Sheridan: if the devil owned Texas and hell, he'd rent out Texas and live in hell.

I hope that old joke will always make Texans laugh and feel a little better not just about the exasperating weather—its wall of heat and stifling humidity—but also about our erratic gardening experiences. Texans who haven't quit their gardens, after years of "E for effort," evince the spirit of the early settlers in our rugged state. Gardening Texans try and try, and they don't give up. They are determined to make their hardscrabble "earth say beans" (to borrow Henry David Thoreau's buoyant phrase).

What follows are some of my own gardening adventures as well as those of others who shared their outdoor- and indoor-plant fixations with me. They and I obsess over our favorite plants. Like lured pollinators, we are mad about certain plants, and some of us (if we are still clearheaded enough to be honest) have been driven a bit crazy by the plants we are crazy about. Never mind that our beloved plants are not biologically designed to make us go bonkers. It happens anyway.

In fact, the history of plant lunacy is long. During the seventeenth century, when tulip mania gripped Europe, there were people who ruined their personal lives and families simply to own or financially speculate on the latest sensational petal striation stemming from the newest virus-infected bulb. During the nineteenth century orchid fever struck England, which also endured a fern craze. Not that this sort of history matters much for addicted plant-lovers. Clearly, for a lot of us there might as well be no such history. We just can't learn from it.

I wonder about the peculiar hold plants can exert on me and other people. I am always drawn to books—and there are many more of them than might be imagined—that delve into this little-understood fixation. The bad news is that their titles are not reassuring. They refer to "madness," "lunacy," "obsession," "fever," and "fraud," while insisting at the same time that what they offer is a "true story."

There will, I imagine, be plenty to hoot over in this book. That would be good, I think. "If you want to tell people the truth, make them laugh," Oscar Wilde sagely advised. My hope is that such truth-laughter in this book might soothe and aid the beleaguered spirits of other gardening Texans.

I am old enough not to flinch at confessing to being flummoxed by nature—coping with its impish waywardness in the guise of "sky flushes," soil erosion, withering drought, scorching heat, unworkable plants, marauding wildlife, unruly pets, and even a looting daughter. Being beaten by nature is hardly the worst admission. Natural forces have thumped me, all right—sometimes sooner, sometimes later (remember that sad lilac). It feels inevitable, like aging itself. Since I am still gardening, I must still be "crazy" about all of it.

The stories told here are about pushing back against gardening challenges, embracing gardening constraints, rethinking gardening possibilities, and learning to care most about those plants that exhibit a can-do spirit in our Texas yards. In the course of my gardening adventures, I (with the stories of others) have zeroed in on some plants and strategies that worked. In these instances we got nature to "say beans" enough times to keep our obsessions going—in my case for almost half a century in Texas. And what better vengeance against nature's tilted "house odds" than to recall and share some of the winning streaks? If I am lucky, these stories will be at least entertaining. If I am doubly lucky, they will prove useful, too. I think of these retellings as casual conversations exchanged among odds-savvy buddies or neighbors sympathetically supporting each other during our mutual gardening endeavors.

When Things Go Sideways

1

Backyard Upheaval

Sometimes while gambling in nature's casino, we catch a break and seem to be on a winning streak. But things can eventually go sideways—and hardly on a small scale. It doesn't have to be as dramatic as a tornado or a hurricane or a flood. It can happen as a steady attrition, a subtle losing streak that takes a while to recognize. And when you do at last wake up to discover that you can't smell the roses, it's uncomfortably late in the game.

In the Beginning

When we moved to our present home in Oak Hill, the area was already losing its identity as a drive-through small town along Highway 290 heading from Austin to Pedernales Falls State Park. Oak Hill still had an enormous amount of undeveloped, rock-strewn land that my wife Catherine and I often explored. The town was also known for its numerous native live oaks, a volunteer fire department, and (later) its own newspaper, but it had been rapidly changing after its annexation by the City of Austin. During the following twenty years, most of this older Oak Hill would vanish beneath a tsunami of home and road construction. The old live oaks that had given the area its appropriate name would steadily shrink despite their City-of-Austin status as "protected," "heritage," and "legacy" trees. City ordinances, it turns out, do not delimit designs by the Texas Department of Transportation. One remaining historical vestige is Convict Hill Quarry Park, a two-acre tract that we and other local volunteers cleared and transformed into

Oak Hill cut

a natural recreational area. Several other larger preserves also remain at present, including one located behind our backyard.

In-ground gardening has never been easy in Oak Hill. The biggest issue is the lack of dirt. Oak Hill has powdery grit, rocks, and boulders instead of dirt. Water runs through this porous earth as rapidly as it does through a sieve. It is the fastest-draining "soil" we have ever worked with. It seems a miracle that, over centuries, live oaks had made such an enduring presence here as well as (initially at least) some sycamores and a few spectacular black walnuts.

The fenceless rear of our newly acquired property in Oak Hill opened onto extensive hardscrabble fields as far as our eyes could see and beyond. Much of this open terrain consisted of exposed loose rocks with small weed-islands dotting the landscape here and there. There were sundry native grasses, prickly pears, twist-leaf yuccas, Christmas chollas, mustang grapes, and nasty greenbrier ("gotcha vines"). That was our property, too, bizarrely described as "a yard to die for" in a realtor's brochure before we bought the place.

A Yard to Die For

This phrase is still a joke between my wife and me. The preposition "for" struck us as terribly off-kilter. A "yard to die in" seemed more apt. It wasn't just the occasional rattlesnake. It wasn't just the sparseness of vegetation. It was also the sheer prospect of what would be physically required of us to transform this rock-rubble where only scattered weeds grew. Our new, rust-hued backyard made us think of the inhospitable stony terrain of Mars. Before we knew it, we were referring to it as "the dead zone," a phrase we still use when remembering our earliest encounters with that backyard.

I found myself mentally partitioning the yard into imaginary sectors. I would sweat away at one sector at a time, I told myself. First, though, we had to build a wooden fence—partly to discourage (hardly deter) pesky wildlife from entering and partly to discourage our adopted venturesome huskies from wandering off. Trying to set posts for this long fence was not an encouraging undertaking. It required a pneumatic drill, went on forever (it seemed), and left me with a starker sense of just how hard our boulder-transformation project was going to be.

Once our property fence was up, I mentally tagged a southwestern corner of the backyard as a husky-free zone where new plantings could establish themselves unmolested by canine digging. I installed an attractive wrought-iron fence (with a gate) around this southwestern segment.

Inside this protected zone, building up was the only way to go. So I wheelbarrowed in a huge quantity of topsoil mixed with compost and organic matter. I spread this mixture over the entire husky-free zone and also fashioned several dirt mounds arranged in a semicircle. Some of the mounded areas were defined by stacked flat stones. Most of the plants we tried on and around these berms did very well, including (among others) several arborvitae (restricted to one side of the semicircled mounds), Texas sage, rosemary, and various trailing lantanas.

We also created a stepping-stone footpath within the dog-free area and built a roofed and latticed arbor with seats for viewing the planted berms. We mounded more dirt, which was irrigated (hardly adequately) by long links of drip hose and retained by a running border of pavers placed roughly parallel to the wooden property-fence. In this margin we grew, among others, rose of Sharon, flame acanthus (hummingbird bush), yaupon holly, primrose jasmine, and a white-flowered climbing rose (*Rosa banksiae*) that eventually sprawled over the arbor and the privacy fence. Once planted, miniature lilyturf (*Liriope*) and mondo grass (*Ophiopogon*) spread easily on their own to produce an appealing groundcover that looked particularly attractive as they edged around and between the stepping-stones.

We are especially partial to varieties of lilyturf species (*L. muscari, L. spicata, L. gigantea*), which are easygoing but extraordinarily resilient evergreens looking like grass. Sometimes they are labeled as monkey grass. Not a grass, liriope is a fall-blooming perennial that is boundless in its sturdy year-round performance. We prize its white- or lilac-hued floral spikes and cute berries, and we are grateful for its wide range of cultivars. Yet we most appreciate liriope for being pretty, unfussy, durable, and evergreen.

Tongues in Trees

Next we pondered the heart of the yard—basically a southwardly exposed barren wasteland scorched by the blast-furnace sun and heat. It literally hurt our squinting eyes to look at it without sunglasses, even from the house's lightly tinted windows.

While there were a dozen magnificent escarpment live oaks thriving in our front yard and one at the rear corner of the house, our backyard was treeless. We wanted trees there too for their beauty, but also as a practical investment, binding the earth and keeping our home cooler during summer. We hoped, as well, that our trees would contribute to air-quality, which has been measurably deteriorating as home-construction, road-use, and denaturalization have surged in the Austin metropolitan area. Large trees might not be xeric, but many are precious oxygen factories of incalculable urban-eco value.

When reflecting on this benefit my mind recalls a strange image: "tongues in trees." It appears in William Shakespeare's comedy *As You Like It*: "this our life, exempt from public haunt, / Finds tongues in trees, books in the running brooks, / Sermons in stones." In memorable imagery Shakespeare refers to those contemplative moments when we sense some personal meaning or lesson seemingly relayed to us by nature.

This is an old idea that never grows old. In a letter written centuries before *As You Like It*, Abbot Bernard anticipated Shakespeare's thought: "You will find something more in forests than in books. Trees and stones will teach you what you can never learn from teachers." As a retired university educator, I wince a bit at that sentiment, but I do know where this once widely read man is coming from. It's a place familiar to gardeners who treasure their plants for so much more than only radishes and turnips.

It's a place familiar to today's ecologists, too. Don't be oblivious to nature, they urge. Pay close attention and decipher what nature teaches us about our past, present, and future course.

In an increasingly warming world, trees have taken on new importance by reminding us not only of their grand position in the scheme of things on our planet but also of the impact of our own history on them specifically and on nature generally. So today we have been hearing more about the importance of forests in offsetting carbon dioxide, the predominant greenhouse gas.

Claims for counting on "carbon offsets" are often too simplistic, unfortunately. The science on this matter remains complicated, not least of all by the fact that some trees emit more volatile organic compounds than they absorb. But it is true that at varying rates, depending on the species, trees photosynthetically store carbon extracted from

Backyard trees

atmospheric carbon dioxide. Trees intervene in climate regulation in other ways, as well, although my point here is that in our present moment we are, so to speak, hearing the "tongues in trees" differently because of questions about global warming (whatever the cause).

We are also hearing more about the origin of trees, "when vegetation rioted on the earth and the big trees were kings," in Joseph Conrad's memorable words. It is easy to feel a sense of wonder over the recent unearthing of the top portions of *Wattieza*, the oldest known tree in the world. From a fossil forest near Gilboa, New York, we now have a glimpse of this ancient arboreal ancestor—a peculiar-looking, twenty-six-foot-tall fern-tree with droopy fronds instead of leaves. Leaves would come later, as would so much else so precious to us on our planet, whether we think about it or not.

Let There Be Trees

Considering what to plant, we took note of the trees in neighborhood yards (spindly redbuds, fragile Bradford pears, twiggy peach trees, decrepit cottonwoods, whippy Arizona ashes) as well as in nearby wild fields (old live oaks, scraggy hackberries, dying sycamores, and prickly Ashe junipers—a lot of Ashe junipers, especially on former ranchland). Of course there also were chinaberries and Chinese tallow trees, fast-spreading and problematic freebies not worth keeping.

We considered planting more live oaks in the backyard, but they grow slowly and are vulnerable to oak wilt, a disease that was already killing trees less than a mile from our home. Gorgeous Shumard red oaks (*Quercus shumardii*) were tempting. We actually had bought one but tossed it after learning that red oaks apparently play a role in the spread of oak wilt. More arbor diversity, we hoped, was a better long-term bet. We were dreaming of easy-on-the-eyes shade from well-spaced trees with wide-spreading crowns touching each other.

When trees were sale-priced at a nearby nursery that autumn, we purchased a number of nonoak species suitable to local conditions. Our intention behind this shotgun approach was to let the trees show us what types could excel in our barren backyard. Sturdy cedar elms (*Ulmus crassifolia*), fast-growing lacebark elms (*U. parvifolia*), and colorful Chinese pistaches (*Pistachia chinensis*), it turned out, would rule. (Chinese pistaches, incidentally, were promoted by the City of Austin then and are currently designated as a Texas Superstar by Texas A&M AgriLife Research,

Autumnal Chinese pistache

but some, including the City now, consider the seeding female trees to be an invasive nuisance.) Surprisingly, a golden raintree (*Koelreuteria paniculata*) took hold, too, and grew tens of feet high in our backyard.

Eventually we propagated some seedlings of the winners. Over time the southwardly exposed backyard became wondrously shaded with plenty of dappled settings. We could actually look at the backyard without wincing or donning sunglasses. The yard, deck, and house were cooler, too, and birds moved in, including white-winged doves nesting in a cedar elm. A desert cardinal (pyrrhuloxia) couple laid claim to our backyard and returned to it every spring for about eight years.

Other creatures moved in, too. One weekend I was cutting away mustang grape vines, which every summer cross over the wooden fence separating our backyard from the nature preserve. The tough vines attempt to strangle and smother our border plants beside that back fence. On this occasion a sudden brief commotion erupted in the tree shading me, and then, equally suddenly, a living mass fell out of the tree, missed my shoulder by inches, and landed at the edge of my shoe. It was a rat snake with its mouth embedded and its coils ever more tightly constricting its rodent prey. The strangling took a few minutes, enough time for me to photograph the ugly episode. The snake, incidentally, did not like my few-inches-away presence (or being photographed) and, after the rat was certainly dead, abandoned the corpse to me (thanks, buddy!) and speedily slithered off into the preserve.

Our neighbors and guests—discreetly kept in the dark about the backyard arboreal escapades of our local rat snakes—have marveled at our towering backyard trees. The trees were so different from adjacent and nearby vacant, rock-strewn backyards still in their original uncultivated state. In our view, of course, the trees were nothing less than majestic. We appreciated them even during winters, when their lack of foliage allowed for maximum light and warmth while the sun hugged the southern horizon during that time of year.

Shock of the New

We planted some more border plants, including Texas lilac chaste-trees (*Vitex agnus-castus*) and crape myrtles (*Lagerstroemia ×faurei*). Next we targeted the southeastern backyard corner, where we built another arbor—this one to support an enduring 'Tangerine Beauty' crossvine (*Bignonia capreolata*). Nearby, along the eastern line of the privacy-fence, we would eventually assemble a glasshouse (for succulents) with a background of tough bamboo (now also on the local list of invasive plants).

We were making progress over the years—or so it seemed. Then things went sideways.

It's not that I was naive about nature at that time or about progress, which at my age seems a philosophical concept open to serious debate. I already knew that nature always has the final say in our gardening endeavors. What I did not anticipate, however, were years of record-breaking drought and heat with record-setting consecutive stretches of triple-digit weather.

These drought years also saw necessary but withering one-day-a-week watering restrictions, with prescribed hours, combined with prohibitive tiered utility pricing and substantial fines for watering during barred times. Automatic sprinklers throughout our yards might have made a difference. They would have made it easier (if no less financially costly) to work with the allotted watering hours permitted on one specified day each week. As the drought dragged on, our drip-hose and sprinkler arrangements were not up to the maintenance task in the backyard, even when the dogs were confined to their spacious, shaded, fenced-in compound to prevent them from digging and becoming "mud puppies." Little could be done about our

Drought-stricken dog-free zone

powdery earth, which retains no moisture. Then there was the fact that too often we were not at home on our designated watering day. So slowly but surely we began to struggle with how to maintain our front-yard and backyard landscapes despite their ample shade.

During high temperatures, carbohydrate production (photosynthesis) simply stops in many plants. In relentless hot wind many plants also lose more water from their foliage than their hydraulic systems can replenish, no matter how much you hydrate their roots. In heat and drought, an overabundance of leaves becomes a liability for nondesert plants, which then self-protectively shed foliage. If drought and heat are prolonged, some plants go dormant prematurely. But dormancy works as a lifesaver only up to a point; death is close by if nonsustaining environmental conditions don't return to normal.

Eventually, the backyard lilyturf stalled and went dormant, most of it slowly dying over time. The once-resilient honeysuckle along the wrought-iron fence withered and eventually died. No more morning glories or hyacinth bean, either, although the star jasmine (*Trachelospermum jasminoides*) soldiered on while benefitting from fence-shaded roots. With their vibrancy diminished, too, the trees shed leaves and twigs daily. It was hard to help them because their canopy was so wide and the drip-line rule (indicating where to water the newest roots under the widest branch ends) has not been a reliable guide in my Texas experiences with trees.

With the loss of groundcover and with diminishing canopy resulting from leaf- and twig-shed, sunlight was once again scorching more and more of the gritty earth beneath the trees. Mulch could intervene only to some extent, and some mulches are dangerous to pets. We had been using hardwood-type mulches here and there. These mulches are easy enough to keep in place.

We avoided cypress-type mulches, which are notorious for preventing air-exchange and also for preventing water from reaching the ground. In fact, cypress-type mulches have been shown to impede plant growth. I had been an advocate of pine-bark mulch until a recent study by Bert Cregg and Robert Schutzki at Michigan State University revealed discouraging results for this cover, probably because of chemical impact. On the other hand, I have been told that commercial nursery plants in the South are routinely and successfully grown in composted pine bark. Perhaps pine-bark compost performs differently from pine-bark mulch.

Whatever the final verdict might be about pine-bark mulch, the fact is that many plants (black walnuts, black locusts, hackberries, and sugar maples, to name but four) engage in the biochemical (allelopathic) suppression of the health of nearby plants. While mulches in general have been shown to measurably benefit garden plants, some mulches can still release competitive allelochemicals. Then these chemicals might inhibit growth hormones (especially in the roots), blocking protein synthesis and preventing photosynthesis in other plants. I have witnessed, over several years, an older pecan tree (*Carya illinoinensis*) bend farther and farther away as if from the "bad breath" of a younger lacebark elm (*Ulmus parvifolia*) and also observed a sturdy yaupon holly (*Ilex vomitoria*) "retreat" similarly from a delicate primrose jasmine (*Jasminum mesnyi*). I have seen decomposing (not blanketing) hackberry leaves "poison" and eventually exterminate conventional turf.

Allelopathic interaction is also something to possibly consider before adding coffee grounds to a garden bed or container. In their native habitats coffee plants leech caffeine into surrounding ground to fend off beetle larvae, slugs, and germinating plants. As Thor Hanson has explained in *The Triumph of Seeds*, "coffee beans know how to kill off the competition—they release their own herbicide, clearing a tiny patch of ground to call their own." It is true that coffee grounds can loosen compacted dirt and very slowly lower soil pH for some acid-loving plants, but not all acid-benefiting plants benefit. Coffee grounds, for instance, have a negative effect on tomatoes, Professor Jeff Gillman has observed in *The Truth about Garden Remedies*. Fresh coffee grounds can actually interfere with various acid-preferring plants' ability to absorb nitrogen because vegetable matter releases nitrogen only when it is decomposing, as in a compost pile. Coffee grounds should be aged for some time before application, which will still amount to a trial-and-error experiment.

So not all mulches or soil additives are equally advantageous. Covering our entire sloping backyard in mulches was never a practical option, especially with dogs in the picture. Our trees were very tall and their roots extended widely, well beyond our yard's boundaries, where they had burrowed beneath the scorched raw ground of the preserve and our neighbors' unmanaged land. So beyond limited hardwood-mulched areas, our backyard earth got hotter, drier, and more compacted—all bad news for our beautiful tall trees.

And the dry granular earth was also eroding. Every day the desiccated surface of the ground was being easily blown away by hot wind, kicked away by the snowshoe paws of our huskies, and even washed away when it (rarely) rained or when we legally watered. Some of our neighbors' unmodified hardscrabble yards had now become deeply rutted with runnels, sometimes with large portions washed away during brief but intense and gouging rainfall. The roots of our big trees prevented that in our case, but even so we were facing a truly bitter irony: during our recent years of prolonged drought, rainfall and watering could have a downside if they contributed to soil erosion.

As hard and embarrassing as it was for us to admit, our once-flourishing backyard was reverting to its original "dead-zone" condition. As boulder edges and some tree roots seemed to be slowly emerging from the ground, the surface level of the yard was actually sinking before our eyes. Grit was getting into the dogs' fur and onto our skin and shoes, and frequent hot southern winds blew it into the house. Our local environment had dramatically changed, and now our backyard demanded another radical intervention if we were going to preserve anything from our first intervention. Somehow the erosion had to be stopped, our trees rescued, and our peace of gardening-mind restored.

Second Time Around

Once again Catherine and I thought about installing an automatic watering system. But it was a bit late in the game for that, not to mention that our rock-and-boulder and (now) tree-rooted landscape would present considerable challenges to belowground installation. We were aware, as well, that at this point in time runoff from any watering system could contribute to ground erosion in our sloped backyard. Nor could we ignore citywide water rationing, with expensive pricing tiers. Although the ever-growing number of Austin residents somehow managed to reduce their water consumption by 17 percent per person between 2006 and 2013, from 2006 to 2014 their water rates had nonetheless surged by 123 percent. City predictions currently indicated an additional 31 percent increase during the next few years, not to mention the looming threat of officially predicted new "drought rates." In fact, even as we were considering how to address our yard situation, the Austin Water Utility department was forecasting a stage 3 citywide ban on automatic watering.

Whatever we decided to do, we wanted to keep in mind that our backyard had "impervious cover limits" designed to protect the Barton Springs Edwards Aquifer. These limits (which we support despite probably being "grandfathered") meant that most of our new interventional landscaping project should permit rain to get into the ground, where it could seep downward. Even without these restrictions, the sheer number of the widespread tree roots we were trying to aid would require that most of our project remain pervious to water.

Getting Stoned

Since our backyard groundcover of lilyturf and mondo grass had (after a long successful "run") mostly failed during the drought and heat of recent years, we turned now to inert groundcovers: tons of river rock, cut limestone, retaining-wall blocks, patio stones, pavers, and pea gravel. Most of these materials would (as needed) have to be delivered to the front yard, the rest managed with our pickup truck. We were looking at months of labor ahead, and we were weighing strategic issues, such as managing the substantial drop-off (slope) in our backyard, which at one point (by the glasshouse foundation) formed a steep natural rain-sluice. Perhaps the hardest trick to pull off would be for Catherine to figure out how to combine these very different materials into an overall attractive pattern.

Just as I had partitioned the yard into imaginary sectors for our first pre-tree landscape intervention many years before, once more I found myself planning our project in portions. The easiest part to picture stretched from side-fence to side-fence along a roughly horizontal line that included a raised peninsula created by a limestone wall I had built previously. This targeted area also encompassed the space beneath the porch ramps and ran parallel to the entire back wall of the house. A dozen or so feet from the house we positioned limestone blocks in a curved pattern. These would serve as a retaining wall, an edging accent, and also our first step-down device to accommodate slope. We covered the ground between this limestone barrier and the house with good-sized river rock.

River rock is pervious to water but not easy on feet or paws. So Catherine came up with a design using foot-friendly, interlocking Canyon patio stones. Starting at the bottom of the back-porch ramp, these patio stones would run rightward (to the yard gate) and leftward (to a fig tree and a fenced-in dog compound). No cement or mortar would be needed, only water-pervious decomposed granite for interfacing the heavy patio stones, locked in place by their own weight and by surrounding river rock.

The other, even larger side of the retaining limestone margin was more challenging to plan. During our first landscape intervention we had "built up," but those mounded border and outlier berms had proved inadequate against the latest Central Texas weather patterns. We decided to build still higher, though not as problematically high as the Tower of Babel. We settled for a large centered plant island made up of stacked (unmortared), curved retaining-wall blocks to be capped by a single layer of mortared Old Town Blend Holland pavers. This island would be completely open to sunlight from its southern side, and it would be filled with a huge amount of good dirt.

Over the years I had built a number of curved walls out of limestone rock, blocks, or brick. These projects have always been a slow process requiring the patient hefting, chipping, cutting, positioning, and leveling of one large stone after another. For me, working with stone amounts to more than mere labor. Retainer-wall building has also always been a prolonged break from the usual hustle and bustle of everyday life, a meditative encounter with slowed time—just me, the next stone in hand, and the measured emergence of an appealing pattern. The pleasing and durable curves of a finished rock wall seem to defy the "resistant" blockish nature of each individual stone. Something surprising emerges whenever "flowing" elegance is wrought from such hard and obdurate material.

The plant island required time to configure and construct, but the last stage of our stonescape project was much harder. Catherine chose 16"× 16" yellow Belle Cobble Concrete pavestones (attractively scored with concentric arcs) that she arranged (in uncemented units of four) around the plant island. Each of these units alternated with open-cell squares that were margined by the Old Town Blend Holland pavers similar to those topping the retaining-wall blocks of the plant island. We then filled these margined open-cell squares with colorful pea gravel.

Keeping everything level, maintaining the running pavestone pattern (four joined squares or appropriate fractions thereof), and managing the occasional "step-down" to compensate for slope presented us with some challenges. Even so, the only place we had to

New growth in a plant island

use a little mortar was around the base of one lacebark elm where the eroded ground angled down too much for us to do otherwise. In a few places, usually to manage drop-off, I hammered into the ground either landscape pins or upside-down galvanized hurricane ties to keep a few pavers from moving out of position.

Sticks and Stones

Our second backyard intervention was finished in 2012. We do not know, finally, how much money or time this project took. Let the word "plenty" suffice. We preferred not to anticipate exactly what the project would require but, instead, kept to our usual practice of just starting with our design and then making headway until a project is completed. Our result won't appeal to everyone or qualify for an HGTV profile, although I will mention that I lost weight and achieved a lower LDL cholesterol score.

The next year, 2013, was another record-setting year for Central Texas drought and heat, amounting to (according to the Austin Water Utility department) a situation worse than the decade-long drought of the 1950s. By the end of 2013, according to the Lower Colorado River Authority (LCRA), Central Texas had endured seven successive years of drought and experienced the second-lowest river- and stream-flow into the Highland Lakes.

Nevertheless, during 2013 (unlike previous recent years) the newly "stoned" trees in our backyard did not shed leaves and twigs. There were no broken limbs, and the "stoned" trees and bushes continued to look vibrant throughout the summers of 2013 and 2014, when the federal government designated my county and the adjacent ones as natural-disaster areas due to drought. In 2015 nearly three months without rain and a brutal August of relentless triple-digit heat, including a succession of blistering days at 105 degrees, hammered the plants in the island but never fazed our trees.

Our widespread stonescape, it has turned out, is the ideal mulch for our trees. It has kept tree roots cooler and protected them from soil erosion by foot traffic, wind, and water. The stonescape has also conserved water by minimizing moisture loss by wind, runoff, and evaporation. Moisture clings to the stones and slowly seeps around them and through the seams of adjacent pavestones to enter the ground. The trees have even sent tiny roots upward to touch the stones, especially the pea gravel.

While our huskies no longer track grit and mud into the house, we do still have some weeds to manage, more so in the surface-strewn river rock than in the more deeply pocketed pea gravel. At the outset of the project we had not attempted soil solarization over such a sizeable project area of already dehydrated and compressed soil. This technique of using black plastic and sunlight to exterminate grass and weeds also kills covered tree roots and crucial beneficial soil bacteria. As an organic technique, in my opinion, soil solarization works best in small spaces that can easily be brought back to life by adding compost and other additives.

We had already learned plenty from others' efforts to prevent weeds from sprouting beneath their hardscapes. There's black landscape fabric, the expensive kind that the pros use, which seems to work fairly well for the most part. Some inventive homeowners had tried shower curtains, vinyl tablecloths, pool liners, and even carpets beneath their river rock. None of these approaches help tree roots. And rain from "sky flushes"—those brief but incredibly intense downpours that have deeply rutted our neighbors' unmanaged backyards—pool in these impervious weed blockers and wash the rocks out, occasionally moving them into the street as far as a block away. Layered newspaper is more pervious, but only works for a short while as a weed blocker and, once saturated, actually serves as a seed-starter medium.

Since so much of our southwardly exposed backyard had already been naturally solarized by sun-scorch, most of our stonescape weed issues have come not from below but from above. No underlying weed blocker can stop the germination of avian- or wind-borne seeds finding a wonderful haven in the damp, cool, shady clefts between the rocks and pavers.

The lovely trees we saved by installing a rockscape became the chief culprits in spreading seedlings among the stones beneath them. Opportunist elm seeds take hold quickly, sending roots quite deep while still out of sight among rocks and stones. By the time these seedlings appear, they are nuisances. That's the bad news. The good news is that despite being nearly a foot long, elm-seedling roots are not widely branched. So these plants can be entirely extracted by hand, one at a time (regrettably), after a substantial rainfall.

A Speckled Rockscape

So I weed, and most interlopers pull free easily enough and (with the notable exception of trumpet creeper [*Campsis radicans*]) don't return. Actually, I have become more laid-back about a rockscape dotted with some low-to-the-ground green here and there—a mixed-media artwork, as it were. I am reminded of a story, told by Benjamin Franklin, about a man who wanted an ax head polished perfectly on both sides. He hired someone to undertake the difficult task, which then stretched on interminably. The would-be perfectionist ax-owner, frustrated and impatient, eventually was willing to accept the tool as it was. "I think I like a speckled ax best," he finally told the worker—and himself. Me, too, I think: I have come to like my green-speckled rockscape just fine. I can live with it being less than perfect.

I am not quite at that point with the plant island, however. Building even higher was an improvement, yet results have remained mixed despite good soil, mulching, and watering. The island might seem an excellent site for growing veggies, but voracious local wildlife—a subject I'll return to later—would have changed our mind within a single season. We've tried to grow veggies here many times before, in the ground and in containers, and we know the sorry score. Even our acorn squash was chewed.

Instead, we planted a variety of vertical-type plants, including various ornamental grasses. In 2013 the grasses in particular sputtered and then went prematurely dormant by end of July. In 2014 and 2015 various cultivars of Chinese maiden grass (*Miscanthus sinensis*) performed less than ideally, and (surprisingly) the purple fountain grass (*Pennisetum setaceum*) barely resprouted. The highly successful island plants include clumps of foot-high 'Emerald Goddess' lilyturf (*Liriope muscari*) and African iris (*Dietes bicolor*), both stalwart evergreens that have remained vibrant and have also bloomed despite ravaging weather.

A South African perennial well adapted to Texas, African iris has always been a top-notch performer for us. In part-shade, its evergreen blade-like foliage forms strong tallish clumps providing muscular vertical features that enhance bare locations. Its creamy-yellow (rarely white) flowers are marked by three orange-ringed, purplish spots. This floral pattern has led to this perennial's nickname: butterfly iris.

There are two other close South African relatives of this drought-tolerant plant: *D. grandiflora* and *D. iridioides*. Unhelpfully, all three are called African iris or fortnight lily, which can be confusing at a retail outlet. The blooms of *D. grandiflora*, which we have recently added to the island, have white petals ("falls"), each with a bright yellow stripe and also a centered crest of faint purple petals. So far their foliage has performed as well as that of *D. bicolor*, though their flowering has been less prolific and more dependent upon watering. Except for their delectable flowers, all three of these African iris species are deer-resistant—not that deer are a problem for us inside the fenced perimeter.

Not Just Any Roses

We opted for roses for the four outer island-loops. Roses matter to me. When I was a child in urban New Jersey, there were two retired sisters next door who converted their entire tiny patch of backyard into a ring of roses. They labored devotedly with magnificent results each year. They made abundant gifts of cut roses to my mother. I am sure they thought she loved getting them and apparently never sensed her less than enthusiastic, succinct "thanks."

My mother was no fan of flowers inside her home. "They make such a mess," she would complain when their petals began to drop. Those roses nonetheless made a lasting visual and olfactory impression on my younger sister and me, and I simply had to have a bush of my own in 1970, when my first home was completed in what was then considered the northeastern fringe of Austin.

I cannot recall how I chose that first rose. It was a bushy, small-leafed floribunda that produced myriads of "double," pale pink, scentless, button-sized flowers. It didn't take long before they covered an entire chain-link fence receiving afternoon shade from the house. Over time, I came to realize how lucky I was in my initial trial-and-error choice. Some of my neighbors had planted roses and were struggling with a number of problems, including few blooms, defoliation, spindly branches, and fatally desiccated plants.

I can't take much credit for my good fortune with that first rose. Like my neighbors back then, I did not have ready access to information about what it takes to grow roses well in Texas. In fact, I have another rose, a years-ago gift that (notwithstanding its wicked thorns) I have moved with me from house to house. I still live with it—a potentially cute, tidy, disease-resistant and cold-hardy 'Ballerina' (introduced in 1937) that unfortunately has never fully realized its full beauty at any of our homes.

Cute, tidy, disease-resistant, and cold-hardy are all good features, but in Texas we need roses that can particularly take plenty of heat and humidity—in short, Southern "old garden" roses. "These are the ultimate time-tested plants, rediscovered after surviving decades in old cemeteries . . . in dilapidated small-town yards . . . and at abandoned homesteads," according to Michael Shoup.

In 1983, with the help of other "rose rustlers," Shoup founded the Antique Rose Emporium in Brenham to reintroduce these forgotten but still vigorous varieties capable of performing like enthralling divas in our Southern heat. Shoup's enterprise was more than a commercial venture. It was also a dedicated pursuit of the true identities of these "lost" roses. Shoup's updated, beautiful book, *Empress of the Garden*, is a must-have for Texas gardeners seeking the best insight into rose varieties that perform gorgeously in our state.

We chose black-spot-resistant and repeat-blooming Knock-Out roses, which are lightly scented and express a delicate beauty. These hybrids are Texas-tough because they have shrub-rose genes in their mix, particularly "Katy Road Pink" (as it was temporarily called after being "rustled" on Katy Road in Houston). This Southern rose was later marketed in Texas under its present cultivar name, 'Carefree Beauty.' After gorgeous spring displays, our Knock-Out roses become leggy and almost leafless during the worst part of summer, when they also stop blooming and look as if they are singed. Then their bare thorny stems remind me of desert cholla-type cacti (which, some have suggested, are post-*Pereskia* descendents of West Indies roses). Usually, however, our Knock-Out roses live up to their reputation as a Texas Superstar by rebounding quickly and bursting out in flowers again by mid-October and then often through most of winter. They don't require deadheading unless you are a compulsive tidier.

Looking Ahead

All of our rescued backyard trees are deciduous—a plus during winter, when their lack of foliage allows for maximum light and warmth while the sun hugs the southern horizon. Leaf-shedding trees meant, however, that we had to overcome our aversion to leaf-blowers. A leaf-blower became essential for cleaning up autumnal debris from our rockscape. We considered user reviews and selected an inexpensive, low-noise, and lightweight electric blower. It has worked perfectly. Sometimes, too, due to paw-traffic, a little of the pea gravel needs to be swept off the pavestones and back into their paver-margined cells.

I am still thinking about how to get the island plants to look more like my ideal image of them there. So far, I am not satisfied. Maybe some of the grasses will do better in possibly more clement future years. The margins along the stoned fence line and in the dog-free area also need more attention. But whatever we decide to do about these matters, that work will be easy compared with the two backyard interventions that have gotten us to this point in our backyard. As for the trees, they have been rescued and continue to grace our yard with their priceless shade and majestic beauty.

For *now*.

2

Going to the Dogs

Our adopted huskies, as expected, have never liked being kept out of the off-limits area we dubbed the dog-free zone. That was especially true whenever there were squirrels, opossums, rats, raccoons, or other animal intruders there. Sometimes the huskies would vigorously twist their heads looking from us and then to the trespassers—repeated, silent, excited "signaling" gestures contesting a prohibition that simply makes no dog-sense. Even so, although they could have easily jumped the honeysuckle-covered, wrought-iron fence around the exclusion zone, they never did. Well . . . at least that we ever knew about.

Over the decades that we have companioned with dogs, not all of our huskies have been so quiet. I recall a few times at a previous home in north-central Austin when we heard yapping from the yard. There was no doubt which dog was yapping, where she was, or why she was there. Snack-seeking Nikki would bull through our garden's chicken-wire fence and then get trapped inside as well as snagged in our thorny blackberry bushes. (I don't remember why we didn't have a thornless variety.)

Gardening with dogs can be much more prickly than a canine berry-heist gone terribly wrong. Over the years our adopted huskies have consistently proved themselves to be yard demolition teams. They're inexhaustible, know no bounds, and really like what they do. A *lot*.

None of them have ever been obedient by dog-trainer standards, and all of them have been true-to-breed willful to the point of orneriness. Their minds move in darkness, someone knowingly said. And they have their own preferences about backyard landscaping—an egregiously messy work in progress that no rational gardener would like.

They love to make craters reminiscent of the foxholes of World War II. These craters are large enough to cool their bellies and, sometimes, deep enough to somewhat conceal their bodies, curled as if tucked into soft snow. Sometimes all we could see were a snout and a pair of pointed ears seemingly perched slightly above dirt level. At night we couldn't see the craters at all, making for treacherous going for us even with a flashlight.

Sure, our particular pets are unemployed medium-sized working canines rambunctiously making work for themselves. But other dog breeds, large or small, can be just as devilish in the yard. In five minutes their digging, chewing, and trampling can ruin a landscape feature that took five years to shape. Pooches seem instinctively to like the garden best when it is "going to the dogs."

So gardening with dogs is something we have had many years to think about and experiment with. I'll tell you about one particularly memorable misadventure after sharing some saner suggestions.

Doggone Compromises

Is there any hope for people who don't like these doggone results but who also insist on having both dogs and a garden? Sadly, there seems to be no perfect win-win solution. All the same, here are a few compromise strategies that helped us make gardening with dogs less stressful.

Since even the best-behaved pooches remain dogs at heart, it's

Two huskies during plant-island construction

best to give up notions of lush flower beds along any fence or wall in their play area. Dogs can't resist searching for buried treasure in the aromatic loamy earth around plants. Telling them "no" in that setting simply makes no sense to their nose or brain, and it's likely they will conveniently forget that particular sound (which you thought was a meaningful word) once your back is turned.

If Fido is a digger, then planting sturdy shrubs, purchased already large, is a better option than border plants vulnerable to trampling and excavation. Arborvitae, Burford holly, primrose jasmine, Texas mountain laurel, and especially pomegranate have worked for us as sturdy in-ground selections that have withstood canine misbehavior.

More fragile plants, such as salvias and rosemary, can be grown in hefty, three-foot-high containers positioned along a wall or fence. If big dogs are tempted to bury prized possessions in these pots—Kodi, one of our queenly female Siberian huskies, buried her treasures there— pea-gravel mulch or a screen can be placed over the dirt surface.

Grass along a fence or wall doesn't fare much better than a flower bed. As they protectively patrol property borders, dogs quickly create unsightly bare-earth racetracks. Hard to miss, the resulting and erod- ing ruts are an unnerving sight to any landscape enthusiast.

With a little dogged creativity it is possible to transform this eyesore into an attractive landscape feature. As mentioned previously, we eventually covered the backyard with stones and pavers. Before that project we relied on a less backbreaking and expensive solution. We set stepping-stones in an appealing pattern along their paw-paths. These stones can be plain or elaborate, set closely together or arranged at intervals, but they should be embedded securely into and level with the ground. Dogs actually discern such spatial definitions, and they will use a stone- or paver-defined path if it tracks their original one.

Mulching a raw dog track is not usually a successful tactic. Shredded wood decomposes over time and is compromised by wind, rain, and paws. Cedar mulch splinters have injured pet footpads and stabbed tongues. If ingested, the splinters become life-threatening. A type of gravel might work, but some look unsightly and most are easily scattered by canine traffic or pawing. Dogs carefully step around river rock if they can avoid it.

Rocks Are Your Friend

Large ordinary property rocks—the excavated kind you otherwise never know what to do with—can also play a role in resisting canine wear and tear. Just as pea gravel protects container plants from troweling paws, large rocks from the yard or purchased molded blocks (arranged in a pleasing pattern, if possible) thwart escape tunnels under fences and other kinds of canine mining beneath property-line shrubs. Eventually, matured foliage downplays the visual impact of whatever is beneath property-line plants.

Dogs love to fashion little dens beneath border shrubs. In these shaded niches they find fascinating critters and also cooler hideaways for summer siestas. Since many plants in our state are sustained by shallow roots—even our deep-rooted trees have extensive shallow roots—it is important to safeguard the ground beneath shrubs and along drip lines (the ground beneath outermost branches). Root disturbance and exposure can be especially critical when plants are young or stressed by heat and drought.

Unless gardening-center stepping-stones or pavers are used, it takes some ingenuity to form an attractive pattern with random-sized rocks from your yard. This is particularly true if these rocks encircle newly planted young trees located in the midsections of a yard. The good news is that rocks, strategically stacked over spread-apart lower ones inside and around the well of a berm, do not impede the slow growth of grass or a groundcover but do keep dogs away from the fresh soil of a newly planted tree. As the groundcover or grass spreads beneath a new planting, the uppermost rocks can be removed and the larger rocks can be replaced by smaller ones.

Think of this maneuver as outfoxing Rover. Generally, dogs do not notice that a rock barrier is diminishing over time. With luck it is possible to get to the point where all of the rocks can be stealthily removed from a tree base now protected by grass or (better yet) a groundcover, such as lilyturf.

Separate Enclosures

Vegetable or flower gardens can be protected by an attractive wrought-iron fence erected around an isolated segment of the yard. That was our preferred option—our so-called dog-free zone. Covering the fence of this restricted area with the vines of coral honeysuckle (*Lonicera sempervirens*) and Virginia creeper (*Parthenocissus quinquefolia*), among other Texas-native possibilities, adds to its effectiveness as a barrier. Another possibility is silvervein creeper (*P. henryana*), a gorgeous Chinese version of Virginia creeper.

Alternatively, dogs can be given their own space—our own second-best option—in which to create the mess they love. Consign a shaded portion of the yard to a fenced-in "run" designed just for them. Big-box hardware stores have easy-to-assemble chain-link panels just for this purpose.

Some dogs tend to object to a compound, especially if you insist on closing the gate with them locked inside the enclosure. One of ours learned to flip up the latch to open the gate. To our huskies the "grass" is always greener on the other side of any fence, and in this case they are right. Their space is what they made of it, while our enticing green space is what we have made of it and then protected from them.

Many dogs can be placated easily by gifts of long-lasting, food-filled toys restricted to only when they are in their pen. Then they will beg to be in their own space—unless you happen to have pooches simi-

Shaded dog area

lar to our female Siberian huskies, who simply don't respond to food rewards.

The doggie playground, incidentally, will quickly become cratered and devoid of greenery. Unless you enjoy wincing, it's best not to look at it. We avoided that issue by using pavers to cover half of the dog compound. Then, in the other half of the pen, we built deck-like flooring, including segments at varying heights that included a large rectangular "house." Huskies, like many other breeds, love a variety of elevations in their playscape, especially a flat roof to climb and then rest on as they cool their dangling paws in the breeze. Unlike our huskies, many dogs will actually use their deeply shaded, igloo-like doghouses.

As for the misadventure: it had to do with a backyard foundation-patio at a previous home. Roofed and tree-shaded, that patio was a favorite space for our dogs. The always-dusty and rough concrete damaged their fur, particularly at the leg joints. So we decided to cover the entire patio with artificial turf. That required a lot of patience, cutting, alignment, and gluing, but the end result appeared seamless and looked great. It felt good to our feet, too, and the dogs liked it.

Rain—normally a blessing for the gardener—sent that project sideways. It turned out that our dogs, who had never urinated on the concrete patio, preferred to relieve themselves on the artificial turf rather than get their feet wet while off the patio. We didn't catch on right away to their changed behavior. After all, they ask to go out and, routinely, we simply let them out. Then they come back. What's to think about?

Over time, though, the new drift of things caught up with us, especially once the entrenched humidity of summer set in. Then the patio reeked endlessly. We could smell it from the kitchen. No amount of hosing sanitized the artificial turf. A day would come when I would denude the patio back to its original gritty condition.

Whatever strategies are tried, gaining a dog's respect is the bottom line in managing canine behavior in the yard or the house. I try to say that with a straight face, despite living with headstrong huskies who always have their own ideas about everything. Plenty of attention, training (good luck!), and exercise, as well as utter consistency in day-to-day directives, are crucial in fostering a dog's pleasure in pleasing you, even when you are not at home. "No" must always mean "no." Then gardeners and their dogs can achieve *détente*.

At least *much* of the time.

3

Free-for-All at the Fig Stop

Fig trees (*Ficus* sp.) are really easy to grow in Texas, and they bear an amazing amount of fruit. They are attractively ornamental in appearance, too. They are so easy to grow that many of us plant them in our yards without much thought. There's more to figs than meets the ordinary eye.

We call figs fruit because they look like fruit. But they aren't. They're inflorescences, a pretty-sounding word for plant structures bearing a number of flowers on a series of stems. The fig tree's hidden tiny flowers actually bloom *inside* these hollow structures we call figs. Technicalities aside, we're still going to refer to figs as fruit.

Fig Secrets

A clandestine drama ensues inside the common figs native to southwestern Asia and the Mediterranean region. Certain species of female wasps, which coevolved to pollinate and enable seed growth in various wild figs, wiggle through a bract-protected opening so small and tight that the insect's wings break off as she enters. That's okay because she's not going to need them anymore. In fact, she's never coming out again.

Inside the fig the wasp accidentally fertilizes some seed-producing female flowers with pollen she has carried since she was born. She also lays eggs in other, nonfertile female flowers found inside the fig. Then she dies.

Male wasps hatch, fill the inflorescence chamber with enabling carbon dioxide, fertilize the emerging females, and then chew a hole in the fig wall. But the escape-way is not for them. Their extraordinarily short life is over.

Their winged sisters, on the other hand, benefit from the release of carbon dioxide through the male-chewed opening. These young female wasps collect pollen from the male flowers now blooming inside the fig and then pass through the wall outlet to venture off into the world. Their mission: to find another fig of the right kind to enter.

Knowing this hidden drama might make figs seem more mysterious and the eating of figs a far less familiar experience. The fact is, however, that ordinarily our commercial figs today are propagated by cuttings from female trees with a mutant gene. This unusual gene makes these ficuses parthenocarpic—meaning they form and keep their "fruit" to maturity without fertilization. No wasps are needed at all.

Many years ago we bought a fig tree for a mere dollar during an end-of-the-season garden-shop sale—its cultivar tag missing by then, of course. We planted it up close to our family-room wall, where it eventually hid a portion of the ugly backyard foundation (built very high due to yard-slope). It has thrived for years in the built-up soil in the stoned-in, three-foot-wide retainer I constructed along the entire south side of the house foundation.

Fig roots do not threaten foundations, and our large-leafed tree, annually ripe with fruit, has always been spectacular to view from the now-dappled windows of the family room and master bedroom. Sure, when figs drop from high up, they make a mess on the patio stones below. And yes, when the lightweight, slightly curled, fuzzy leaves detach, they tend to stick in the rake tines or frustratingly "sail" rather than assemble when approached with a leaf-blower. They are, simply, more difficult to clean up than most other fallen autumnal foliage. Even so, dropped drupes and big leaves do not compromise the easy-care status of a fig tree.

Avian Hordes

There are many cultivars of figs, and they are definitely not equal in quality. Richard Ashton, a fruit-tree propagator in Brownwood, has identified 'Texas Everbearing' as even tastier than the longtime Texas favorite 'Brown Turkey.' He also recommends small-fruited 'Celeste' for eastern and northern Texas.

Our mystery-cultivar figs, it turned out, are not the tastiest. Perhaps they are in too much shade from other trees or perhaps they are just what they are. When fully ripe and weeping, they are still slightly "green," at least to our tongues. But they cook up nicely and make a wonderful preserve, especially when blended with maple syrup, vanilla-flavored agave sweetener, or raw honey. (Processed honey, beekeeper Jack Mingo has reported, often has been heated to a high temperature and forced through ultrafine mesh to remove pollen traces that otherwise could identify offshore sources contaminated by "heavy metals, pollutants, antibiotics and other chemicals not approved for human consumption.")

Since our figs are not the best for snacking, we don't give them away. We tend to leave plenty on the tree for thirsty birds craving a sweet treat during the long dog days of summer, when local wildlife find moisture hard to come by. The figs ripen and weep in July and August, which are particularly hot and droughty months. As the thirsty birds flock to our fig tree, we get to watch them (only several feet away at most) from the windows in our master bedroom and family room.

Juvenile mockingbird eating figs

Sometimes they come in hordes and noisily raid the fig trees all day long. That would be a problem if we wanted all the figs, and this is something to think about when planting a ficus for harvesting. Then you might want to deploy some nets to safeguard your figs. Otherwise, the thirsty birds might keep at it day after day until the tree is stripped bare of fruit. We root for the birds, which sometimes raise their young in the fig tree, too.

Unwelcome Marauders

We are less enthusiastic about the other marauders drawn to that ficus. The worst offenders are squirrels, which push out the birds and gobble up as much fruit as they can grab. They take hasty bites of the fruit, which they also discard partially eaten. I will have plenty more to say about squirrels a little later, but suffice it to say here that they don't appeal to us as cute furry critters welcome to the smorgasbord any more than they are invited to our attic.

Then there are the conniving thieves who wait for the cover of darkness—nocturnally foraging opossums, raccoons, and rats ready to argue with each other over fig turf. There have been nights we have been awakened by ruckuses raging through our fig tree. Once, around 2 a.m., in a fit of pique, I went outside with a flashlight and broom to break up a nonstop free-for-all of some kind between noisy raccoons and an oblivious possum.

One weekend night, around 9:30, something worse happened. A skunk "bomb" silently exploded, filling the backyard porch with an eye-searing stink that invaded the family room, too. Since Siberian husky Simka was patrolling outside in the dark, as is her usual prefer-ence until bedtime, I rushed out to make sure she was not the skunk's target.

She was, though. She was rank, with obviously sore eyes, but she was still unwilling to relent in her dogged effort to put an end to the invader. The skunk had been tempted by the fallen figs beneath the tree and was braving Simka's territorial control. There had been no rain for over six weeks, and that skunk had found an amazing amount of downed succulent treasure it refused to abandon.

A thought flashed through my mind, a recalled bit of advice long ago from a friend hardened from our mutual exposure to academic politics. "Never get into a pissing contest with a skunk," he had warned.

Not that Simka was open to any advice. Trying to clean her in the front yard that night was hard. Like some other breeds, huskies generally hate handling, intensely, and what ensued was a slippery wrestling match as we tried to clean her. We flushed her eyes with contact-lens solution. Then we washed her with vinegar and water (which seemed only slightly effective) and then again with a mixture of hydrogen peroxide, baking soda, and oil-cutting dish detergent and dog shampoo. The best (if still limited) results came from an acquaintance's recommendation: Woolite.

She turned out *mostly* refreshed, except for her head. She stank in our bedroom that night, where she routinely sleeps on the floor. It takes a bit of mental management to go to sleep in a room smelling from a fig-filching skunk.

A Fig Stop Unskunked

Come the next morning, she still smelled enough for us to notice. Outside, the area around the fig tree remained deeply rank from the oily skunk spray. I tried to track the skunk by smell that morning, while also relying on the huskies' indication of where some intruder had entered. (Nothing gets by them; they even know exactly what restaurant we have visited and what their take-home treat should be.)

I found the skunk burrowed beneath the slab for our air-conditioning condenser. It had moved in during the three days we had been away. From the trace of tail that I could see, the creature appeared to be small. I thought, perhaps, it was one of the several tiny skunk kits I had seen weeks earlier beneath a boulder in a preserve area around the corner. But I was wrong. It was the size of large cat when it emerged in response to my flushing it out with a hose. In retreat, it showed me where it had entered the yard. I boarded up that surprisingly small space as well as stoned in the stinky hollow it had made beneath the small slab.

Skunks are built to dig under or scramble over things. This one had also squeezed beneath the chain-link barrier we use to keep the dogs away from the potentially dangerous condenser (which once chopped up a rat snake). The fallen figs had lured this intruder, but in fact skunks can climb somewhat, particularly trees (such as our ficus) that are angled diagonally.

So you know what you are in for if you plant a fig tree. It will be easy

A plentiful fig yield

to grow and it will be beautiful. And you will get plenty of fruit. It's a carefree plant except when a skunk shows up and creates a fracas resulting in a lot of nongardening work.

And—count on it!—if you plant it, "they" will come. A considerable number of incorrigible animals will be eyeballing your figs from the first onset of fruiting.

What follows will be much more than mere eyeballing.

4

Incorrigible Banditry

My neighbor (several doors over) was telling me about the big ones that got away. Not fish, but tomatoes. There were five of them, large and dark green, hanging upside down in a grow-bag extended from her deck. And then suddenly they were gone, just like that. Not quite gone, though, she said. There were chunks of bitten, smashed, and scattered tomatoes nearby, as if imps had brainlessly delighted in tearing apart the unripe fruits.

She was familiar with the culprits' hooligan pranks in the past and, this time, she had actually seen them running from the splattered scene of the crime. She had hoped that the suspended grow-bag would be beyond their reach. But she "had underestimated them again," she sighed stoically.

She is not alone in her trouble with garden bandits. Tales of critter-begotten woe are widespread in our neighborhood, which includes stretches of nature preserves. My neighbor's yard and mine border on the same wild terrain, which harbors raccoons, rats, opossums, and birds that easily and predictably raid our gardens. We have skunks, foxes, and coyotes, too, but our fences usually deter them. The deer are gone now, though (unexpectedly) there has been a recent uptick in neighborhood encounters with porcupines.

Chief Mischief-Maker

The chief offenders, of course, are squirrels—the very scoundrels who made off with my neighbor's tomatoes. Sometimes they can seem to be cute furry creatures given to playful antics, but for gardeners and

Fox squirrel

homeowners, squirrels are often an infuriating and costly menace. It's grating for some of us that the little mischief-makers are celebrated not only during National Squirrel Awareness Week (in October) but also on Squirrel Appreciation Day (January 21).

Homes are chewed on, attics invaded, electrical wires stripped, trees debarked, buds bitten off, gardens dug up, veggies sampled, bulbs excavated, and container plants knocked about or shredded. All of this is not just about sustenance and a place to live. It's about teeth. Squirrel teeth grow six inches every year and are kept healthy, short, and sharp by nearly nonstop chewing on just about anything.

Has squirrel trouble gotten worse over the years for urban gardeners in Texas? Scientifically, I can't say. But there's plenty of anecdotal evidence that squirrel mayhem has worsened. And I feel it in my bones.

If you plant trees, you get nonstop squirrel highways. If you plant gardens, you get noisy squirrel food courts and playgrounds. Probably our recent years of drought are a factor, but the most likely reason for squirrels' apparent increasing impact on our yards is the rapid pace of urban development. In Central Texas, for example, squirrels are steadily losing their natural habitats, including a substantial reduction in rodent-controlling predators.

Crime-Stoppers

When it comes to protecting gardens from squirrels, so much has been tried, so little has worked. It's humiliating that this rodent's pecan-sized, six-gram brain is so hard for us to outwit.

Success stories are few and painfully limited in scale. For example, keeping tree limbs pruned to at least ten feet from a home discourages rooftop squirrel mayhem. Also, two-foot-wide metal bands or a circle of empty plastic milk jugs, ten feet above the ground, can be secured around trunks of fruit or nut trees. But these interventions work only for non-fig-type tree trunks with branches inaccessible from rooftops, nearby trees, and the ground.

Mulching alone, we learned the hard way, will not prevent squirrels from filching fall-planted bulbs. Bone meal, no longer touted by bulb enthusiasts, actually lures squirrels. On the other hand, blood meal, a good source of nitrogen for bulbs, seems to thwart them. Unfortunately, blood meal invites excavation by other animals, including cats and dogs (both squirrel enemies). Although there are squirrel-repellant products to coat bulbs before planting, their overall effectiveness is difficult to determine. Planting bulbs with both hot-pepper flakes and nearby garlic cloves has worked for some.

Just blanketing the ground with red-pepper flakes failed when we tried it. So did my use of stationary plastic snakes and owls. Other disappointed gardeners have complained about the brief effectiveness of bad-tasting and awful-smelling commercial powders and sprays (including fox and coyote urine) designed to deter squirrels. Mothballs emit a mighty stink but dissipate quickly and (even when inside cloth sacks) can be neurologically lethal to pets and other animals.

A tree spray combining cayenne pepper, chili powder, Tabasco sauce, and Murphy's Oil Soap is recommended by Jerry Baker in *Bug Off!* I have kept squirrel chewing at bay by dabbing various home surfaces with cayenne-peppered glue dried overnight.

Seeing Red

Baker also suggests tying red balloons to branches. Two of my neighbors (Pat Pringle and Susanne Ross) had good results with tomato decoys: red Christmas ornaments and eye-hooked, red-painted golf balls attached to plant cages. Willis Beam in Killeen swears by cut pieces of Irish Spring deodorant soap suspended in pantyhose as a short-term deterrent.

Some gardeners surround their in-ground plants with pinecones and sundry prickly vegetation. Their goal is to create an unpleasant surface for squirrel feet. But think twice about lava rocks. If ingested, lava rocks can kill pets.

A two-inch mulch of crushed stone discourages squirrels from digging in containers, although many plants will not tolerate the likely lingering dampness around their stems. The area underneath in-ground plants can be covered with a well-secured wire-mesh screen—not chicken wire, which squirrels gleefully yank up.

These admittedly small measures are hardly consoling considering the extensive amount of damage squirrels inflict on the leaves, stems, and flowers of expensive deck and garden ornamentals. Without protective cages—hardly a practical solution—these plants remain vulnerable to squirrel havoc. This includes marigolds, pelargoniums (commonly called geraniums), and other companion plants often said to ward off squirrels. We tried them and lost. While it is true that such pungent plants do not attract squirrels, they aren't spared after more appealing plants have been destroyed. Even hot-pepper plants aren't spared.

Whenever (to my huskies' delight) I squirt squirrels with hose water, the rodents take offense and scatter in vociferous indignation. So apparently a motion-sensor sprayer would deter the blighters—if your nontomato plants can withstand unscheduled overhead hydration and if you have the space and (particularly nowadays) the budget for so much watering.

Some gardeners try to appease squirrels by supplying water and food, especially dried corn. It's a dicey gambit that might result in attracting more squirrels and a host of other unwelcome varmints. Such an effort goes counter to the standard advice to remove squirrel-attracting pet food, barbecues, garbage cans, and bird feeders. Squirrels especially pirate bird feeders. Bill Adler has devoted an entire (funny and wise) book, *Outwitting Squirrels*, to "cunning stratagems to reduce dramatically the egregious misappropriation of seed from your birdfeeder."

Capture and Release

Adler supports capture and release, but in my experience this approach can be frustrating. Live-catch traps do work but are awkward and also attract a wide range of other animals, including possums and skunks. Even worse, as hunted (game) animals in Texas, squirrels are protected by various state and county regulations.

While the Texas Parks and Wildlife Code "prohibits the trapping, transporting or transplantation of game animals without a permit issued by the department," it exempts squirrels "under certain circumstances." "No permit is physically issued for the relocation of nuisance squirrels," Karen Pianka explained to me while she served as the Wildlife Permits Coordinator at the Texas Parks and Wildlife Department. But, she added, whoever transports the animals must carry written permission from the owner of the property where the squirrels are to be released.

Pianka pointed, as well, to other requirements found in the Texas Administrative Code, also referred to as Proclamations. These elaborations of state laws indicate that squirrel traps must be labeled "with the owner's name, street address, city, and telephone number." Also, the traps cannot injure the squirrels, which must be released within twenty-four hours of their capture.

What remains, finally, is the ongoing contest of wits between you and the squirrels—with the little furry fiends possibly adapting rapidly, getting smarter, living longer, and (it sometimes seems) vastly outnumbering you.

5

Not Walden Pond

One year, as the wildflowers of spring gave way to summer's blasting blitzkrieg, the idea of a backyard pond especially appealed to us. With the sun steadily steering toward the center of the sky, it was easy to imagine a water garden as a little oasis of eye-soothing blueness ringed by lush greenery. As a famous Japanese haiku celebrates, a pond can offer refreshing glimpses of nature's spontaneous rejuvenation: "An old still pond: / but a frog leaps / and water splashes."

Wouldn't such a pond be perfect for the dog-free zone?

This was before the Internet made how-to information as easy to access as the air we breathe. Trial-and-error experiment, offset a little by some guidebooks, was the mainstay of so many of our undertakings back then. And this was before water use became an inhibiting regional issue.

Ponding has many rewards, but they come with effort. From the outset there is the matter of whether to hire a professional or to undertake the task personally. Digging a large hole to accommodate a rubber liner or a pond module can be difficult. In our case, a pond installation meant excavating huge chunks of rock. Some we extracted by pulling ropes tied around them. That took a sweaty while, and then there was the challenge of getting the jagged holes into shapes matching the two modules we had purchased and planned to position adjacent to each other.

We ended up rubber-lining the modules eventually. Although we had blanketed the excavation sites with ample sand, leaks resulted from the natural instability of the stony ground combined with the attrition of supporting sand by rain over time. We found out the hard way that the weight of our pond water was substantial enough to press

Pond in the dog-free zone

the ponds so hard into our resistant rocky ground that each plastic module developed a crack.

Positioning Challenges

Because many of their roots are shallow, trees can be damaged by close excavation, which may be a good reason to construct the pond *on* rather than *in* the ground. If an aboveground pond is planned for a deck or yard, selecting a location is still an important consideration. Most water plants prefer full sun, but the flora around a pond may need to be somewhat sheltered. Dappled light or afternoon shade lessens algal blooms and water evaporation, but it also usually reduces aquatic-plant flowering. Also, water gardens located beneath trees periodically fill with leaves, which need to be removed to preserve pond eco-health and appearance.

The decisions do not get easier—but in a good way, this time. A paradise of possibilities awaits your selection of pond flora. Besides a seemingly limitless assortment of water lilies and lotuses, there are "floaters," which have roots not anchored in soil, "marginals," which create dramatic border effects, and "oxygenators," which filter and clean water by competing with algae. Concerning the outside boundaries of the pond, the opportunity for various designs is enormous.

Amount of sunlight and plant size are also important floral concerns. We added long strands of two readily available aquarium plants, fanwort (*Cabomba pulcheri*) and hornwort (*Ceratophyllum demersum*). And then we purchased small-padded water lilies requiring about six hours of daily light. Dainty tropical varieties are cute, but particularly in the northern regions of Texas they probably need to be protected during winter. There are, fortunately, hardy small water lilies, such as the fragrant white-flowered *Nymphaea* 'Gonnere' (which thrives in dappled light) and the brilliant yellow *N.* 'Chromatella' (which sports a crocus-like orange center).

Among the many other attractive aquatic selections, crinum lily (*Crinum americanum*) and lizard tail (*Saururus cernuus*) are worth a second look. These two Texas natives reach between one and three feet in height in only six inches of water, and they display magnificent white blooms in sun or shade. Louisiana iris functions as a gorgeous marginal, too. Don't overlook eye-appealing nonblooming alternatives, including dwarf common reed (*Phragmites australis*) and dwarf papyrus (*Cyperus haspens*). Both give the otherwise flat-surfaced water garden some aesthetic scale.

For a different effect try golden globes and creeping Jenny, both spreading members of the *Lysimachia* family that brighten pond margins with an abundance of radiant yellow flowers. These two cold-hardy perennials bloom in summer, but moisture and light shade are crucial to both of these lovely loosestrifes.

The bright red blooms of cardinal flower, a name commonly attached to three species of *Lobelia*, make a dramatic summer statement when potted or planted along partially shaded pond edges. The actual cardinal flower (*L. cardinalis*) grows to about three feet, whereas its namesake, water lobelia (*L. dortmanna*), barely attains one foot. Both are cold-hardy, unlike red-leafed lobelia (*L. fulgens*), the beautiful tall Southern native (also known as cardinal flower) that might need to be wintered indoors.

Water snowflake garnishes partially shaded pond margins with feathery floral stars in white (*Nymphoides indica*), orange (*N. hydrocharioides*), and yellow (*N. crenata*). Its floating heart-shaped, green-bronze pads provide an extra attraction. This potentially invasive aquatic blooms from spring through autumn but is vulnerable to temperatures below 10 degrees Fahrenheit. Water violet (*Hottonia palustris*), with mauve-flowering lacey foliage, behaves better territorially.

'Chameleon' (*Houttuynia cordata*) produces cute small white flowers from summer through fall, but even more striking are its variegated heart-shaped leaves, which change hue in response to variations in sunlight and temperature. Periodic shade and an inch or two of water over the plant crown help prevent summer leaf-burn. A highly invasive plant potentially capable of surviving North-Central Texas winters, this aquatic should be restricted to pond-margin containers.

Sensitive plant (*Aeschynomene fluitans*), so named because its fuzzy leaves close when touched, adorns summer with intense yellow flowers mimicking sweet pea blooms. Whether grown as a floater, rooted plant, or rock climber, this aquatic spreads rapidly and may require periodic retrenchment. Not cold-hardy, this particular sensitive plant should be kept moist when wintered indoors.

Water lilies tend to be voracious feeders, so be prepared to buy special fertilizer tabs (10-14-8) and a unique tool to insert these tabs into the submerged, root-compacted pots. I was never able to pull these containers from the pond—they achieved an unbelievable weight. Nor could I ever manage to use my fingers to insert the food tabs while I leaned precariously over the water. Warning: attempting this chore can result in a funny home video, especially if you lean a bit too far over the water while trying to monkey with the slippery pots.

Since our ponds were located far from the house, we had no easy access to electricity to power pumps that would produce a continual water flow necessary for mosquito control and a healthy system for fish. Fish require an eco-balanced habitat, including adequate food and aeration. Shallow ponds in particular are not ideal for fish, which require safety-depth levels during summer and winter. Fish can contribute to a healthy water garden, or they can unbalance it. Besides causing algal blooms, they can increase the amounts of ammonia and nitrite in the pond, which in turn imperil the fish.

Whether or not you plan for fish, don't skip the pumps. That was a mistake in our case. Years later we had to give up altogether on our pumpless ponds. And today, unlike our effort many years ago, a pond-keeper can try solar aeration systems instead of finding a safe and attractive way to run electric wires very far from the house to the ponds.

Who Goes There?

A pond is a mighty magnet for thirsty wildlife, and fish make it doubly attractive. We saw raccoons washing in our ponds, often with destructive effects on the aquatic plants. If we had had fish, the raccoons would have hunted them. At some point a neighborhood cat showed up, and if we had had fish that cat would not have been only admiring its "selfie" reflected in the water.

Birds love ponds, too. A reappearing mockingbird loudly sang daily in our water-garden oasis. A pyrrhuloxia couple, those perennial warm-weather guests in our yard for about eight years, hunted for seeds and insects along the pond margins. Ruby-throated hummingbird migrants were sometimes noisy as they defended the orange blossoms of the trumpet creepers (*Campsis radicans*) and the flame acanthus (*Anisacanthus quadrifidus* var. *wrightii*), as well as drained the reddish flasks of the coral honeysuckle (*Lonicera sempervirens*) established along the fences near the ponds.

Butterflies and other pollinators also stopped by. Dragonflies, donned in neon orange or blue, tirelessly hovered over the water in eager anticipation of any mosquito that might have newly emerged in spite of our steady use of Mosquito Dunks to insure the eradication of hatching larvae.

This fascinating natural-history extravaganza notwithstanding, our ponds were no copy of Walden Pond—Henry David Thoreau's idealized oasis. Thoreau was something of a con man who "fudged" and fibbed for a good cause. He had nothing to say about timber rattlesnakes or copperheads, which he doubtless encountered sometime during his lifetime of outdoor adventures. Somehow, as well, the unpleasant visitors to his pond underwent magical transformations. Sure, he acknowledged the "the faint hum" of mosquitoes as they entered through the open door of his hut. But according to Thoreau, these bloodsuckers only sang a Homeric epic "of the everlasting vigor and fertility of the world." Good grief! That's all the mosquitoes did inside his hut? Surely Thoreau's bitten body felt a starker reality about ponds and mosquitoes. If my personal encounters in Massachusetts and Southeastern Texas are typical, skeeters "up north" are not as body-punching wicked as ours, but they are nonetheless decidedly a pain.

Sometimes, I admit, our home ponds could entrance Catherine

and me into a Thoreau state of mind imagining some natural wonderland. Some nights a competitive amphibian glee club broke forth, a pleasant mating cacophony that often sounded like some low-keyed contemporary musical composition. That chorus was comforting to our minds, muzzy with tiredness at a day's end, as we lay in bed at night before the onset of sleep.

But eventually the music stopped, and the silence became loud enough to keep us awake.

One morning, we searched the pond margins for some clue about the change. There were no tiny amphibians on the lily pads. A toad-cave under a pond-edge rock, where we had often spied its large denizen comfortably plump, was now vacant. It was as if every resident amphibian had sung its last song and then deserted this petite paradise in search of another.

Early one morning we spotted an orange stripe winding through the purple-flowered lantana (*Lantana montevidensis*) on a pond fringe. A closer look revealed two feet of an eastern blackneck garter snake. Not venomous, this distant relative of the amphibians had arrived on the shores of our little Eden and had dispersed its choir. No doubt it had enjoyed some of them as a snack. There were other garter snakes, as well, and at least two of them (we have photos!) engaged in poolside

Garter snakes mating poolside

mating. Another time we saw a red stripe smoothly gliding among the lily pads in one of the ponds—a tadpole-devouring ribbon snake.

The pond area now was very quiet both day and night. Even the mockingbird quit slaking its thirst there. Every Eden has its serpent, we sighed, accepting slither-kind for what they are. Begrudgingly we came to appreciate these snakes' odd charm. After all, we consoled ourselves, weren't they more pleasant guests than, say, that thick four-foot creature, with oh-so-many rattles, that we saw a week or so earlier in the field on the other side of our south fence?

As with a fig tree, if you install a pond "they" will come. And they will not always be quite who you expected or preferred when Thoreau-dreaming about your little oasis.

6

Scandalous Unlawning

I was reluctant to mention turf-type grass when speaking about the vanishing-rock trick when gardening with dogs. Although every one of our homes came with a lawn in some sort of condition, we have never been turf admirers.

So at our present home we inherited a lawn. It went the same way as my hair. It was just a matter of time.

Buffalo Blues

Many years ago in Oak Hill we had a front yard entirely covered with buffalo grass (*Bouteloua dactyloides*). It was wonderfully eye-catching, especially when its thin bluish-green blades waved as gently as breeze-rippled water.

Our buffalo grass was doomed, however. It faced northward and was also easily invaded by weeds that were seeded abundantly from nearby wild areas, especially the nature preserve behind our backyard.

Then over time our live-oak canopies grew higher and spread more gloriously wider in the front yard. As evident from our later landscape overhaul project, we have always especially prized trees. In this instance, we had privileged the dozen front-yard escarpment live oaks (*Quercus fusiformis*) original to the land before our house was built. Unfortunately, the spread of those magnificent trees was a success story with an unhappy ending for the prairie grass below.

Another culprit, though, was my neighbor's St. Augustine turf, which slowly but surely displaced our less dominant buffalo grass. Buffalo grass does not stand a chance against St. Augustine or Bermuda grass runners, which invade any space with militant determination. My

Front-yard windbreak

neighbor's lawn inevitably annexed ours, and that's the grass that now roughly carpets portions of our front yard. And I do mean *roughly*.

Perhaps I should be grateful for the patchy gift turf. I want to be, but I'm not. That's why I speak of once having had a lawn. The new front-yard turf doesn't interest me. As far as I am concerned, it's on its own. When I water (as allowed by local laws), my objective is to aid the live-oak tree roots, not the grass blades of the sketchy passed-along lawn.

Not Just a Lawn

What exists of our freebie lawn always looks as if it is having "a bad-hair day." There's no way it will ever be "mown into a softness like velvet," Andrew Jackson Downing's 1840s promising description of the ideal American lawn. Even if we had zoysia instead of St. Augustine, we simply don't want to be the caretaker of a "proper" lawn. We can't find cuteness or enjoyment in conventional turf, which is just too unrewardingly needy.

I suppose that, if for some reason our lawn were legally required— were we, say, oppressed by some homeowner-association bylaws—we would try a type trademarked as Habiturf. It's a dense native-grass mix developed at the Lady Bird Johnson Wildflower Center, a research unit of the University of Texas at Austin. It establishes quickly and looks respectable as yard turf. Watering and mowing would be less than usual, but still there would be boring upkeep.

It is not just the upkeep that bothers me. Since I moved to Austin in 1969, I have been ambivalent about traditional lawns. They seem frustratingly inappropriate for our climate, especially given increasing heat and drought in our region.

It's not that we are critical of anyone who is obsessed with a typical lawn. We have a wonderful neighbor—you could not ask for better—who gladly slaves over his lawn nearly every day. He feeds, he waters, he cuts, he edges, he rakes, and he painstakingly weeds while on hands and knees. He asks people very politely to please keep their dogs off it. He's thoroughly devoted. Every gardener is prone to and perhaps entitled to an obsession or two. I have my own—more, in fact, than the trees you already know about.

Usually when we purchase a house, *voilà*—there's a lawn in front. Now we're lawn-keepers. That this would happen must have been somewhere in the fine print of the deed transaction papers. Puzzling over this phenomenon in *Lawn People*, Paul Robbins interviewed many homeowners who found themselves in this default post as lawn-keepers. He wanted to explain how "the needs of the grass come to be [our] own." Lawns represent more than most of us realize, Robbins found. Although *Homo suburbia* (a turf caretaker) doesn't know it, lawns encode hard-to-challenge social, cultural, and political meanings reinforced by the economic interests of powerful corporations.

The extensive cost of maintaining nonnative traditional turf is also humorously but trenchantly examined in Ted Steinberg's *American Green*, an eye-opening exposé of corporate exploitation of our lawn mania. The wordplay of the book's title conveys perfectly the close bond between lawn culture and corporate profits.

I'm drawn to such books delving into the "why" of standard lawns and the pressure on us exerted by them. I silently root for the authors of these books. I'm hoping they will reassure me that my turf-indifference is, after all, okay in a world where proper lawns tyrannically rule, often with the clout of local ordinances, homeowner associations, and the raised eyebrows of neighbors.

Unveiling the Turf Mystique

So I delighted in "Why Mow?," the enticingly titled third chapter of Michael Pollan's engaging book *Second Nature*. I found its succinct skeptical history of American lawns to be irresistible reading. After all, I'd rather be reading than messing with my lawn, especially when the act of reading about the seedy backstory behind lawns gives me an excuse to ignore mine.

What Pollan discloses, though, is somewhat unnerving. Since the end of the nineteenth century, he points out, some Americans have branded my kind of indifference to picture-perfect front-yard turf grass as (to quote him) "selfish," "unneighborly," "undemocratic," and even "unchristian." These harsh charges are discomforting. And because misery likes company, I easily fall (while reading online) for sympathetic "click bait," such as "My town calls my lawn 'a nuisance.' But I still refuse to mow it," which appeared one day on the *Washington Post* website. There's no way I am not going to read that.

But Pollan doesn't sweat in the least about blowback as he demystifies the turf mystique. He even tries to let go of his own lawn by transforming it into a vegetable garden. That garden is boldly, even transgressively, bordered by unruly, low-maintenance hedge plants, including forsythia, lilac, bittersweet, and bridal wreath. Good for him, though many Texans will consider different hedge plantings.

Subversive Unlawning

Pollan isn't the only one who encourages veggie gardening as an act of subversive unlawning. So does Heather Flores in *Food Not Lawns*, which contentiously advocates for a politically radical transformation of homescapes. "Practicing ecological living is a deeply subversive act," Flores writes, referring to her belief that turf grass represents a corrupt social, economic, and political state of mind.

She's thinking of the extravagant wastefulness as well as the history of traditional lawns. While earlier Americans spoke of well-kempt lawns as neighborly and democratic, oddly in fact turf grass's still earlier European history began with people of considerable wealth and privilege. Those lawns were status symbols for aristocrats who hired low-income workers to keep up the grounds. Over time the possibility of having a status lawn trickled down to the middle class—for better or for worse, depending on your perspective.

Flores is not the least bit subtle in her "for worse" position. She attempts to arouse a populist, antiestablishment spirit that is supposed to return us to a more healthy and natural way of life. Her book is less a how-to manual than a passionate, sometimes off-putting rallying cry for the conversion of unproductive front lawns into productive crops.

Veggies are not the only unlawning option. The projects recommended by Sally and Andy Wasowski in *Requiem for a Lawnmower* emphasize going native. Replacing a lawn with plants native to a region means supporting wildlife-friendly habitats and water conservation. Going native also means less labor for homeowners as well as freedom from the environmentally damaging chemicals frequently applied to lawns, at greater cost than mere dollars.

More Fun Than Lawn

We have disinherited our inherited lawn in a number of ways beyond simple neglect. There are sections of the front yard where we extracted turf and fashioned raised beds for bulbs and other plants. The brick used in the curved retaining walls of these beds matches the brick of our home. Next to one raised bed, located in front of a living-room window, we planted a native crossvine (*Bignonia capreolata*), which produces enduring evergreen climbers that require virtually no care whatsoever. Rescued years ago from a nearby lot under construction, this crossvine now adorns an arch structure and withstands everything nature throws at it without any setbacks. In early spring it produces an abundance of gorgeous red-throated yellow trumpet flowers.

All year long the view from that living-room window is decorated with the crossvine's vibrant green foliage. It's also a vantage point for observing a variety of small visiting birds, including vivacious tiny tufted titmice. Over time this crossvine does reach out toward the house to attach tendrils to brick and roof. So, yes, we have to trim it back—an easy task requiring mere minutes. Our Texas native crossvine is not at all as invasive or unmanageable as trumpet creeper (*Campsis radicans*), a hummingbird favorite that we allow on sections of the privacy fence.

Crossvine is companionable as well. For late-spring and early-summer blooms, we planted a very tame "mystery" hybrid vine with butterscotch trumpets—another cheap end-of-season purchase with cultivar tag missing—that intertwines on the same arch. The two plants get along perfectly and both clearly have migrant hummingbirds' approval. The trumpet vine needs a few snips to trim back its bare whips during winter, but this plant's leafless stems during that season are completely cloaked by the evergreen foliage of the crossvine.

We also created grassless circles for in-ground and potted-plant combinations and inserted islands of evergreen groundcover, especially star jasmine (*Trachelospermum jasminoides*). Some may simply dismiss this plant as a lowly, even bothersome vine. It is so much more than that when positioned with careful consideration. Extremely tough, this wiry climber will dutifully ornament or hide wide swathes of ugly privacy fences.

Also known as Confederate jasmine, this rapidly spreading evergreen is neither Southern in origin nor a jasmine in identity. It's Asian, but not quite the same plant as close look-alike *Trachelospermum asiaticum*, also (confusingly) known as star jasmine. Both are called jasmines because of the pleasant jasminish perfume of their pinwheel-shaped flowers during spring. We can identify the star jasmine that covers much of our front yard and side fences as *T. jasminoides* because it bears white flowers with faint yellow-tunneled throats rather than the bright yellow-starred throats said to be characteristic of *T. asiaticum*.

At one point we had this groundcover only in an unlawned space between a paved walkway and the house foundation. Since the weedy, long, and narrow strip between the driveway and a privacy fence barely supported patches of grass, it became another candidate for star jasmine. Propagation was ridiculously easy. One day I trimmed the Confederate jasmine vines encroaching on the entranceway pavement. I did not root them in pots or plant them in the ground. I simply tossed all of these cuttings willy-nilly onto the narrow strip and then poured sacks of topsoil loosely over them and watered—overall, a carefree exercise in survival of the fittest.

Within a year that strip between the driveway and fence was well on its way to being covered with star jasmine. Now this plant also blankets the entire expanse of the privacy fence there. A wall of living green, it looks great year-round. But as my tough-love propagation by strewn stems suggests, star jasmine is an aggressive survivor and, once established, will need cutting back now and then. It tries to reach across sidewalks and it climbs trees. At least twice a year I must trim it back.

Growing a Lost Cultivar

In still another deliberately unlawned space we planted something special. A number of years ago, while I was walking through an old central Austin neighborhood of rundown houses, I spotted a slender bowed shrub with a few white flowers. It was obviously a rose of Sharon (*Hibiscus syriacus*) struggling to make do in too much shade and with too much owner neglect. What caught my eye, though, was the pattern and size of its flower petals. They were smaller and more spread apart—wilder looking—than today's rose of Sharons, which are bred to feature well-proportioned foliage and particularly large flowers with close-together petals.

For a brief moment, perhaps, I felt like a plant explorer who had just made a find. I was, in fact, looking at a rose of Sharon from the past, a cultivar no longer marketed in the United States. Long ago it had been displaced by flashier newcomers, such as 'Diana.' I have long shared Katharine White's skepticism about hybridizers' quest for ever-bigger flower sizes. Protesting a growing commercial emphasis on the "Mammoth, Giant and Colossal," *New Yorker* columnist White wrote: "I have never been able to persuade myself that the biggest blooms are necessarily the most beautiful." Exactly. With permission, I made cuttings of the "rediscovered" rose of Sharon and propagated three plants. Planted side-by-side, they are slimly tall now, and every summer all three bloom beautifully in a grassless segment of our front yard. They appear to be 'Totus Albus,' an *H. syriacus* expert told me one day while asking for cuttings for herself.

Our grass-conversion projects included a faux well made up of retaining-wall blocks arranged in a circle and "filled" with bulbs for a number of years and then eventually with three Knock-Out roses. We were most satisfied, however, with a densely planted windbreak, which runs the entire length of the front yard and varies in width between nine and twelve feet—a deliberate unevenness that gives its margin a natural curved appearance. This unlawned windbreak includes two arborvitaes and a Chinese pistache. There are large bushes (fringe flower

A faux well with in-ground spider plants

[*Loropetalum chinense* "Monraz"], rose of Sharon, and pomegranate), medium-sized shrubs (viburnums, hollies, and Indian hawthorns [*Rhaphiolepis* sp.]), and small plants (lantanas, pavonias, salvias, Mexican oreganos, and various other native plants). This greenbelt shields the rest of the front yard and our home from the sights and sounds of the street, and it provides a lush, cool, shaded space for visiting small wildlife, including urban-adapted neighborhood foxes foraging during the twilight hours.

We have a wildlife-friendly segment in the backyard, too—a deeply shaded thicket located behind the glasshouse, where our huskies love to act out their innate lupine fantasies. One afternoon our youngest husky at the time was exhibiting approach-avoidance behavior I've seen our dogs use when confronting snakes. As I hastily approached the thicket, I saw what appeared to be an Eastern screech owl on the ground. It had probably settled on the dimly lit bushes as a relatively cool escape from the blasting sun and heat of that 103-degree day.

Untypically, the husky obeyed my command to leave the scene to me. Actually, she seemed relieved to no longer have to deal with the odd creature. She had been flummoxed by the tiny owl, which was making loud clicking sounds while spreading its wings wide and rotating its head in small arcs. These diversionary tricks made the dog pause over her paws.

"Symph" Serendipity

Our most satisfying going-native addition to the front-yard windbreak initially arrived as "aster" freebies. Despite their long-enduring common names, most so-called native asters are technically not asters any more. They now taxonomically belong to the genus *Symphyotrichum*. While it is not hard to derive a short, catchy pop name from this newer category, the switch to "symphs" is not likely to happen. It is, in fact, still necessary to look for these plants under "aster" in some wildflower guides, and they are also often still labeled as such on market tags.

The Texas natives include annual aster, tall aster, Drummond's aster, heath aster, spread-leaf aster, broad-leaf aster, *hierba del marrano*, rough-stemmed aster (which is rare), bushy aster, white aster, and dwarf white aster, among many others. It takes a good eye, some practice, and perhaps a bit of luck to sort out the identities of these natives, especially since they can easily cross-pollinate between species and sometimes back-cross to produce hybrids that challenge definite identification by eye.

These native symphs are undervalued, probably because of their unwelcome presence as weeds in lawns and plant beds. In ideal settings some can spread quickly during the course of a single year. In no case are their small blooms as flamboyant as the New England aster (*S. novae-angliae*) and the New York aster (*S. novi-belgii*), the sources of so many market cultivars. These cultivars are not ideal for droughty Texas, and I have sometimes thought of them as "asters courting disasters." Their humbler but florally prolific Texas cousins deserve a closer look. They easily serve as appealing niche-fillers capable of cohabiting closely and trouble-free with most other garden plants.

One of our favorites is a persistent wildflower in our Oak Hill neighborhood. It is likely a variety of Drummond's aster (*S. drummondii* var. *texanum*, previously known as *Aster texanus*). Whatever symph these long, slender perennials actually are, we welcome them within the windbreak at the front of our yard by watering them during prolonged dry spells and by dispersing their seed.

They begin to reappear during winter. Often by the end of January

Texas native Symphyotrichum grown ornamentally

Mexican petunia (Ruellia simplex)

their bright green, serrated leaves form tightly bundled, close-to-the-earth "mats" designed to protect the new growth from still more winter weather. At this mid-winter point there is no hint of the tall stems to come during spring.

While this perennial's foliage tends to be widely spaced along the stems, its small lavender-blue flowers are usually stunningly abundant and also include a showy seed stage. As niche-fillers, our native symphs thrive even with long stretches of shade, and they tolerate being ensconced in tight quarters with bigger companion plants.

They are extraordinarily tough, too. During the wicked weather of 2011—reportedly the driest and second-hottest on record for Texas—our wild symphs hung on despite their foliage looking as if singed by fire. With the first meager rain in autumn, a number of them, though nearly leafless, rushed out blooms. They did not look their best that autumn, of course, but they were a welcome pleasure after a year of such dispiriting weather. Symph-loving native bees—what few I saw in 2011—seemed grateful as well for this sudden late-season, grand finale of blooms in the cooler shaded nooks of the windbreak.

A Naturalized Beauty

Another freebie that we cheerfully welcome is Mexican petunia (*Ruellia simplex; R. brittoniana*). Every single one of ours started out as an interloper in our yard. Not every gardener is so grateful to find this territorially aggressive pass-itself-along ensconced in lawns and garden beds. But we are.

Standing nearly three feet high, this Texas-naturalized perennial (which is not actually a petunia) can cast seed several feet from its stems. One secret to Mexican petunia's effortless land grab is its efficiency in utilizing nitrogen and phosphorus. Also, its long narrow leaves adventitiously limit water loss (transpiration) by heat and wind. Despite summer temperatures and drought, its colorful pink or purple flowers can be seen ornamenting abandoned lots and even thriving in the tiny clefts between sidewalk slabs.

We simply move Mexican petunia freebies from where they sprouted to where we want them, including the windbreak and also the bricked-in bed beneath the living-room window facing the crossvined arch. Clumped together, Mexican petunias are gorgeous as a mass or accent plant. Ours remain evergreen, and even those in North Texas tend to show only leaf-tip damage during winter. If these perennials die to ground, their resilient and colony-forming rhizomes quickly recover in the spring.

There are better-behaved, low-growing ruellias, such as 'Katie,' first cultivated by Katie Ferguson in Conroe, Texas. Great for borders, these compact plants mound to about six inches high and one foot wide. Blooming from spring through fall, their abundant flowers usually remain physically close to their foliage. I admit, reluctantly, that the floppy look of these noninvasive perennials has never much appealed to me.

Is there any hope should you prefer the majestic tall ruellias if only they were better behaved? Look for 'Purple Showers,' a sterile hybrid cultivar of *R. brittoniana* (sometimes listed as *R. tweediana*). It is as lofty and beautiful as the seeding variety, and it is equally carefree. Or look for 'Snow Queen,' a tall white-flowered hybrid cultivar of *R. brittoniana*. Hybrids generally reproduce poorly, often not at all. It has been suggested as well that even nonhybrid white-flowered ruellias are not known to escape.

Incidentally, the invasiveness of bad-boy Mexican petunias—the ones we like just the way they are—can be impeded by planting them in poor but draining soils and then keeping them dry for as long as possible. It's the availability of ample water and soil nutrients that puts them into reproductive overdrive. If the goal is to keep naturalized Mexican petunias in their place, water them only when they begin to wilt. However, this practice also considerably limits flowering. A better approach is to grow these ill-mannered ruellias in containers. They are wonderful candidates for pots placed on a bright but partly shaded deck, where they aren't likely to become a nuisance.

If you have native symphs and naturalized ruellias in an inappropriate flower bed, think of them as serendipities—out-of-the-blue gifts that just need to be transplanted to a more suitable setting where they can sprawl a bit and bloom. That's what we do with these free, pretty, durable and no-maintenance options for replacing shaggy sections of our struggling and unappealing traditional lawn.

The presence of weeds does not always mean that something has gone sideways. Some so-called weeds are really worth keeping.

Chapter 6

7

Turning Inside Out

It's no secret that recent years have been record-setters for drought and heat in Texas. When the National Atmospheric and Oceanic Administration updated its thirty-year "climate normals" in 2011, its statistical report revealed that Texas had gotten measurably hotter overall and particularly during the previous decade. Climate scientists speculate that this pattern of increasing high temperatures and dryness will continue in our state, and so far their prediction has been accurate. As I write this, the last ten years have pegged a new heat record for our state.

When plants wilt in such record-breaking heat, our gardening spirits tend to flag, too. During such a long siege of high temperatures, some of us might be tempted—at least in our minds—to unload our spade and trowel at the next garage sale. That's understandable but hardly comforting.

Alternatively, to adapt a cliché, if we can't beat the weather, maybe we can join it. That's what Mark Simmons suggested. As a restoration ecologist for the Mueller Prairie project in Austin—thirty acres of Blackland Prairie reclaimed from a defunct airport parking lot—Simmons has maintained that we should adjust our perception of what is an acceptable appearance for home landscapes. Forget green, he told Anne Raver of the *New York Times*, "We have savannas here, dark evergreen trees and grass like Africa that turns brown in the dry season. That's the nature of plants."

Seriously? Forget green and get used to crunchy brown? And for how many months of every year? I just can't do it. Yucky brown is not an option for me.

To be fair, Simmons is primarily referring to lawns. As I have already indicated, I am all for reconsidering conventional lawns in Texas. When it comes to my landscape in general, however, I am stubborn and want to find ways to have green, plenty of green, all the green I can get and can efficiently and economically maintain despite heat and drought.

Going Emerald

One way I get that green and keep it is to raise ordinary houseplants outdoors. Going tropical with outdoor houseplants lets me turn our months-long heat wave into a gardening plus.

I am not referring to zone pushing—gambling with houseplants as in-grounders vulnerable to our winters. Instead, I dot my home landscape with houseplants in moveable containers. For at least eight months of every year a variety of potted tropical houseplants ornaments unlawned niches in our front yard: scheffleras, dieffen-bachias, syngoniums, pothos, philodendrons, cordylines, dracaenas, soft-leafed yuccas, and even kalanchoes. Unlike zone pushing, there is no gamble in my going tropical in this way. Instead, it's a sure thing with an outstanding payoff.

Say the word "tropical" and a host of popular exotic plants comes to mind—Chinese hibiscus or murraya, for instance. These are primarily valued for their flowers. While some of my neighbors are zone pushing these and other popular tropicals as in-ground plants, I keep them in containers moveable by dolly to locations that are both ideal for the plants and also for highlighting their contribution to the landscape.

But these particular tropicals are not usually considered house-plants. Houseplants are tropicals typically kept inside, where their prolific foliage (featuring striking shapes, structures, veining, variega-tion, and size) enhances room ambiance. They are also kept indoors to protect them from climatic injury.

However, being indoors is hardly always ideal for them. Their vigor can be compromised by problems resulting from too much or too little light, hot or cold air blown from vents, uneven soil moisture, too much or too little humidity, leaf-burn, and defoliation. Pests seek out stressed plants, and too many indoor houseplants can be easily stressed.

When they are moved outdoors from spring through autumn at our home, our houseplants perform better than they do indoors.

Indoor plants grown outdoors

They flourish in the outdoor heat and humidity, and their lush foliage gracefully redeems shaded niches otherwise decimated by high temperatures and drought.

This has been particularly true for our three potted scheffleras. Indoors they tend to yellow, shed leaves, and attract mealy bugs. When outdoors for most of the year, they radiate emerald-green energy—as gorgeous an effect as any houseplant lover could wish. And this rich

Blooming donkey ears kalanchoe

Cautionary Notes

Is there a downside to our pursuit of persistent green when so much else is turning yucky savanna-brown? Of course! Like alternating current, life's plusses come with minuses.

The biggest minus in our scheme inevitably occurs with the first weather forecast warning of temperatures falling into the thirties. Then all of our houseplants must be moved into our windowed garage, where we install agro-lights. That dolly-assisted move is a hassle, and the garage gets uncomfortably crowded and messy, I admit, but ultimately such bothers are small tradeoffs for eight months of tropical beauty in the front yard.

A word of caution, though: watch out for plant buddies after moving the potted plants indoors. It's always a surprise to find a sporty anole, possibly a bit bewildered, leaping among the tropical houseplants overwintering in the strange new world of a garage.

One December, while writing a gardening article at my desk, I was startled by a sudden, nonstop crunching sound nearby. It was as disconcerting as it was distracting. I looked around and then under my desk, but to no avail. Catherine heard the sound too and started searching the room. Eventually we focused on our vibrantly beautiful and miniature calamondin orange plant serenely stationed next to a window behind my desk chair.

Noisily and rampantly chomping away on luscious green leaves were two orange dog caterpillars (*Papilio cresphontes*). It wasn't night and it wasn't spring or summer, the proper time and season for them. Yet, fostered by the misleading heat of our home, here were two future giant swallowtail butterflies swiftly devouring our cute orange tree, which had spent the previous hot months outdoors. When we attempted to remove them, the caterpillars "threatened" us by thrusting their fiercely orange osmeterium, which looks like a snake's forked tongue. It was quite a convincing performance that gave us pause despite our supposedly being smarter than the birds thwarted by this defensive device.

Little creatures can set in motion more gardening drama than their meager size would seem to enable.

Troweling for Answers

8

Dad, Can We Grow a Christmas Tree?

Many of us value solitude when gardening. While getting our hands dirty, we are also performing cleansing work within our minds. Gardens are always about more than the sum of our physical actions there.

But sometimes sharing certain garden activities with others is just as satisfying. In the late 1970s my preschool-aged daughter frequently joined me in our vegetable patches. She eagerly learned to carefully collect, wash, and prepare cucumbers, peppers, squash, and eggplants. Together we canned jars of sweet pickles, enough to last an entire year.

Once, on a lark, we also grew horehound, a sun-loving perennial that thrived in our dry and poor soil in northeast Austin. My daughter and I harvested the herb's abundant grayish green foliage to make candy. Cleaning the pot required some trouble, I recall, while the candy-making itself was by no means hard. Jessica hated the candy, while I was ambivalent. It got eaten anyway.

My daughter was especially enthusiastic about growing green beans. She loved the sight, feel, snap, smell, and taste of them. She may have been the only kid to be so crazy about green beans.

But her favorite self-appointed task was berry-collecting. Each day during berry season she impatiently checked the blackberry canes that we had threaded through our chain-link fence close to the running water of Little Walnut Creek. As the stains on her face and shirt always suggested, it was likely that for each berry she collected in her pail another one had disappeared into her mouth. Strawberries were particularly vulnerable.

My only ally was a skittish little green snake, which apparently liked the 7' × 7' strawberry patch as much as my daughter did. When the insect-eating snake was present, my strawberry yield seemed to increase. Jessica has, she says, some fond memories of her forays into those long-ago gardens, although her recollection of the extent of her berry larceny appears to be as skittish now as the smooth green snake was then.

When gardening these days, Jessica includes her own daughter. Jessica and some of her friends are aware of the New Nature Movement based on Richard Louv's *Last Child in the Woods*, which influenced the creation of the family garden at the Lady Bird Johnson Wildflower Center. Louv suggests that the gradually widening distance between nature and "wired" urban youth contributes to childhood obesity, attention problems, and depression. (As a former educator, let me add the unsettling observation that students seem to be increasingly unaware of even nature's most basic daily patterns.) To address this nature-deficit disorder, as Louv describes it, direct exposure to the restorative powers of nature should support healthier physical, emotional, intellectual, and creative development in children.

Children often respond to gardens with a sense of wonder and delight as beautiful as any flower and as nourishing as any veggie. Children also come with a bushel of questions.

One day, while we were clipping pine needles together to make mulch from a neighborhood postholiday pile of discarded conifers, my daughter asked, "Dad, can we grow a Christmas tree in our yard?" Maybe she was privately wondering whether the season of cheer could be made to last all year, instead of just a few weeks, if only a Christmas tree were growing as a permanent part of our home landscape. In her case, such a thought would not surprise me. After all, when she was a few years younger, she had once asked me to identify a big luminous round object glowing close to the horizon in a clear evening sky. When I answered, "That's the moon," she instinctively extended her hand, palm up, and said, "Want it!"

Returning to my daughter's question about growing Christmas trees at home: Yes, you can! And, yes, we did! Texas is a great place for growing trees with shapes suitable for the Christmas season. Our trees aren't the same as those from the northern parts of our country, but they are trees that amply fit the occasion. That's why, in fact, the Texas Christmas Tree Growers Association lists over a hundred members.

Minimal Effort

The experience of Texas Christmas tree farmers is helpful when thinking about what tree to grow and how to care for it. While farm-raised Christmas trees vary depending on the region, the most prevalent species raised in Texas include Afghan pine, Virginia pine, Arizona cypress, and Leyland cypress—each capable of withstanding our hot, dry conditions.

Don't look for in-ground Scotch pines, Colorado blue spruces, or Balsam, Noble, and Douglas firs at local cut-your-own Christmas tree farms. Although these are the trees traditionally associated with Christmas, they are all unsuitable as in-ground plants in Texas landscapes. If any of them are available at local Christmas tree farms, they are sold as pricey precut, out-of-state imports.

While raising one or more Christmas trees in a home landscape will hardly be taxing, it is likely that some strategic pruning will be necessary to ensure the desired conical shape. Most of the trees profiled here come in cultivars that naturally taper into a conical form. Even so, some tidying is commonly required to maintain, highlight, or sharpen this form. And this little chore can get to be a bit more demanding as the trees grow taller. At some point, well after your children are grown, most of these trees will become too tall to decorate easily.

Despite occasional pruning, the homegrown Christmas trees surveyed here are basically low-maintenance plants. When located in draining, slightly sloped sites with plenty of space and sunlight, they pretty much take care of themselves. They are also mostly resistant to drought and, for years, require no feeding. One thing to keep in mind, however: many of these trees emit breeze-dispersed volatilized organic compounds, especially on very hot and humid days. That's the Christmas tree scent we detect, a smell that is pleasant or unpleasant, depending on each person's disposition. I have met people who considered a whiff of their neighbor's Arizona cypresses on a hot afternoon to be somewhat oppressive.

Trees to Grow

Leyland cypress (*Cupressus cyparis leylandii*) is highly regarded for its lush feathery softness. It may somewhat vary the traditional Christmas

In-ground Leyland cypress

tree look, but it offers compactness and an easy-to-manage height of five feet or so.

Since the soft branches of Leyland cypress bend easily, decorations must be lightweight. But the foliage of this hybrid of Alaska cedar (*Chamaecyparis nootkatensis*) and Monterey cypress (*Cupressus macrocarpa*) does not shed. It also lacks pollen, making it scentless—good news for anyone who is allergic or scent-adverse to conifers.

Another good-news feature of this tree is that it can be raised as an indoor container plant. This approach requires much more attention than an in-ground planting. Overwatering can lead to root rot. Besides excellent drainage, an indoor Leyland cypress needs plenty of southern-sunlight exposure.

When thinking about growing any plant indoors, it is important to keep in mind that today's energy-conserving tinted windows are not the same as the glass panes of yesteryear that allowed windowsill plants to thrive. Similar to the effect of solar screens, these new windows have an impact on growing indoor plants—how much depends on film, tint, coating, or between-panes gas. Apparently in Texas, gray is the most common window tint for reducing the penetration of outside light and heat. Such a substantial reduction of light—up to about 70 percent—poses challenges for the houseplant grower, who now needs to consider the use of fluorescent, high-intensity discharge (not incandescent) or plant-light bulbs.

Eldarica pine (*Pinus eldarica*), also known as Mondell or Afghan pine and often misspelled as "Elderica," is perfect for the laid-back gardener. As a home landscape addition this evergreen grows rapidly with minimal maintenance. Since this conifer excels in droughty conditions—including windswept San Antonio Street in Marfa—it should not be placed in a regularly irrigated landscape.

Its sensitivity to too much water is a plus in economic and conservational terms. Unfortunately, this same trait becomes a minus in East Texas, where mature Eldarica pines too often become fatally diseased as a result of more rainfall than they can tolerate.

Although the long needles of Afghan pine are bristly and its wide limbs are somewhat open—not quite the preferred Christmas tree look—this strong plant will support large decorations. It is the most prevalently grown selection on Christmas tree farms in Texas. While its scent is slight, the tree can get quite tall, and over many years it will likely become impossible to decorate from top to bottom.

A beautiful native of the Southwest, including the Big Bend area, Arizona cypress (*Cupressus arizonica*) is an increasingly popular choice for home landscapes. It's easy to see why. Its aromatic blue-green foliage is especially striking, adding a lacy effect to this tree's appealing overall conical structure.

Extremely drought-tolerant, Arizona cypress is prominently featured at the Lady Bird Johnson Wildflower Center and has excelled in

'Blue Pyramid' Arizona cypress

my Oak Hill neighborhood. Like Eldarica pine, it does extremely well in locations with excellent drainage and so may struggle in East Texas. Since it gets very tall and wide, it needs plenty of room.

The thirty or so available cultivars of Arizona cypress indicate its surge in popularity for home landscapes. For particularly outstanding Christmas tree–shaped selections, look for 'Carolina Sapphire,' 'Blue Ice,' and 'Blue Pyramid.'

We Texans commonly refer to junipers as cedars. Eastern red cedar, which is really *Juniperus virginiana*, is no exception. This native conifer is "the most used evergreen in Texas graveyards," says Greg Grant, a garden research associate at Stephen F. Austin State University in Nacogdoches. This tree is a graveyard favorite because it is environmentally durable and so has long symbolized enduring memory. These are good reasons to plant Eastern red cedar for festive occasions at home, too, especially the Christmas season.

There are Christmas tree–shaped selections of the Chinese juniper (*J. chinensis*), a tough conifer that adapts to both alkaline and acidic settings. But be careful. There are many varieties of this juniper, and most are not conical in form. Look for 'Excelsior,' 'Fairview,' or 'Oblongata,' a slow-grower with a swirling taper.

For a tree already decorated with its own highlights, as it were, consider the variegated 'Aurea' cultivar of Chinese juniper. Or, even better, consider the slim, bright, variegated spire of the 'Swane's Gold' cultivar of Italian cypress (*Cupressus sempervirens*). This densely foliaged twenty-footer never needs trimming and can be grown in the ground or a planter. It needs excellent drainage, ample sunlight (particularly since it is variegated), open space, a hint of soil acidity, and water during dry spells.

Other Christmas tree substitutes include conical cultivars of arborvitae (*Thuja occidentalis*), which have thrived in my various Central Texas yards for decades. It was the Christmas tree I planted for my daughter at each of our homes because this plant is gracefully beautiful, easy to grow, and never too tall to be lightly ornamented (eventually with the aid of a ladder).

In Texas, arborvitae excels best in the northern half of our state, wherever it is colder and wetter than my Austin suburb at present. My arborvitaes have always been trouble-free until recently. Some of my current arborvitaes now exhibit sectional dieback (dead branches) due to environmental stress, particularly paucity of rain. Recent record-breaking years of heat and drought have heavily taxed the shallow roots of these trees in my yard. Some natural cedar flagging may be occurring as well. Still, most of my arborvitae are doing fine.

Since the climate of our Oak Hill home is officially hotter than it was previously, the 'Wichita Blue' cultivar of the Rocky Mountain juniper (*J. scopulorum*) might have been a better option than arborvitae for our present homescape. Featuring attractive silver-blue foliage, this evergreen is native throughout Texas.

Trees to Avoid

Although I have often seen potted Deodar cedar (*Cedrus deodarai*) marketed at nurseries during the Christmas season, it may prove

'Wichita Blue' Rocky Mountain juniper

disappointing. It is cold-hardy in most of our state, but its emerging shape can be unpredictable. There will pruning—probably a lot.

There is still another issue. Eventually, pruning won't rescue this tree from its propensity to droop its limbs, including its trunk leader. As time passes, the weeping look, perhaps attractive in some garden settings, tends to compromise even the conical-shaped cultivars of this Himalayan conifer.

Also sometimes available for the holiday season, Italian stone pine (*Pinus pinea*) will disappoint long-term Christmas tree expectations. It is conical only during its earliest years. Then, in stark contrast to Deodar cedar's weeping manner, the Italian stone pine tilts its branches sharply upward to form a rounded top—which is why this southern European native is also known as umbrella pine.

Take a close look at any cute Italian stone pine available for purchase as a potted Christmas tree. Odds are that it already needs retapering, especially at the top. This seemingly small detail reveals that the plant presently looks like a Christmas tree only because of strategic pruning just prior to marketing.

With an Italian stone pine you'll be pruning throughout the holiday season—and hardly feeling merry about it. It's a pretty tree, capable of surviving Central Texas heat and dryness, but it won't function well as an in-ground Christmas tree.

9

How Old Is This Tree?

Children aren't the only ones with garden queries. A homeowner in Garland once asked whether there was a way for her to determine the age of the large cedar elm located at the front of her home. The impressive tree had influenced her decision to purchase the cute home and now she was wondering how old it might be.

Garland cedar elm

Of course, if you plant a tree yourself, then you can calculate its age from the day you put it in the ground—although you will still have to guess how old it was at the time it was purchased in a container. But if the tree was already in the ground well before you became its caretaker, its age will be far more difficult to calculate.

Even so, the age of some tree species can be reasonably surmised, up to a point. The International Society of Arboriculture has come up with a formula for estimating the age of a number of tree species without cutting them down.

Tree-Age Formula

The formula for tree dating is straightforward. First, circle the tree with a measuring tape positioned chest height (4.5 feet from the ground). Bark can interfere with keeping the measuring tape evenly circular, so get help and watch for places where the tape might ride up or down the trunk, which will throw off your measurement. The resulting measurement around the trunk (girth) is its circumference. Next divide this circumference (in inches) by pi (3.14) to derive your tree's present diameter.

Second, multiply this diameter by the tree's "growth factor." A tree's growth factor should not be confused with its "growth rate," which refers to a plant's vertical growth per year. A tree's growth *factor* is derived from scientific study of specific species over time. The International Society of Arboriculture has established the growth factor for about forty tree species (http://forestry.about.com/od/silviculture/a/Estimating-A-Trees-Age.htm).

Redbuds, for example, have a growth factor of 7, while the growth factor for American elm is 4.

Formula Limitations

In a sense this formula is "deceptively" straightforward because even if we were all growing the same tree type out of the forty or so studied species, the environmental conditions for our plants would vary considerably from yard to yard. The soil, climate, rain history, microconditions, and homeowner attention would all differ from one regional yard to another. These differences would have an impact on the growth patterns of even identical species of tree. This is especially true in Texas, with its diverse regions, soils, and weather. And it matters, as well, whether the trees are growing in the wild, in the country, or in an urban setting.

To illustrate this point, there's an episode I sometimes think of as "the case of the five Texas mountain laurels." It remains a frustrating "cold case," however, because my processes of elimination never finally revealed an evident what-done-it.

One of my neighbors had planted a series of five Texas mountain laurels (*Sophora secundiflora*). As native plants, these are sure-

Texas mountain laurels at an early stage

The same Texas mountain laurels years later

fire, if slow-growing, winners in our state when they are planted in well-draining soil. A 2002 study concluded that Texas mountain laurels reach a standard height of twenty feet or so and particularly excel in a regularly irrigated medium of sand, silt, and clay. In early spring their gorgeous bee-enticing wisteria-like flowers fill the air with an agreeable fragrance, which has led some locals to call them lilacs.

It is evident that my neighbor meant for the five plants—all initially about the same size in their pots and planted on the same day—to grow into an attractive, relatively uniform foliage screen offsetting the stark privacy fence behind them. Each bush/small tree was planted the same distance apart from each other and also from the wooden fence.

And yet, despite all the care and planning by their planter, all five Texas mountain laurels grew at different rates over the years, resulting in a line of evenly spaced plants with dramatically uneven heights. Five healthy plants; five wildly varying heights—a far cry from the artistic design hoped for by the gardener.

So what went wrong?

Microclimate variation is not a likely explanation for this particular outcome. Nor is genetic difference, though that possibility can't be altogether ruled out. As their foliage has indicated then and now, none of these native evergreens are unhealthy. They have never been frozen in winter nor defoliated by moth larva. And there is no sign of trouble below in the grass, which looks the same at the base of each of the plants. The so-so grass has not been chemically treated with pesticides, herbicides, or even fertilizer—all of which, incidentally, could inhibit Texas mountain laurel development.

None of the five plants enjoyed any observable major advantage. All shared the same slight slope, a good feature ensuring soil drainage and also possibly benefitting the bottommost plant at first. All received the same amount of sunlight (all day) and rain. There are no underground incoming or outgoing water lines on this side of the property.

Possibly some of them were root-bound at the time of planting and became somewhat girdled in the ground. Several experts, though, now say that being root-bound when transplanted is overrated as a potential problem. Since the mountain laurels are native plants and all were about the same size in their pots on the day of their transplanting, being root-bound seems to be an unconvincing explanation for their different growth rates and sizes. It is true, nonetheless, that transplanted mountain laurels are fussy and often slow to adapt to their new locations.

The frustrated Sherlock in me suspects that the culprit lies below, where I cannot see—in the landfill beneath the turf-supporting blanket of good soil. That landfill includes who-knows-what types of builder's debris and other trash. Texas mountain laurel's "long, sparsely branched root systems"—Jill Nokes's description in *How to Grow Native Plants*—go deep. So possibly some underground problematic chemical combination or deficiency accounts for the strange varied heights of the five Texas mountain laurels.

Their unevenness continues and remains unsolved after two decades, making at least one humbling lesson perfectly clear. Gardeners are artists working with living materials. We may compose with the greatest of ingenuity, but in the end nature rules and often keeps its secrets.

Another lesson, too: even if it were ever possible to derive a growth factor for Texas mountain laurels, that number would not shed much light on the actual age of each of these multibranched small trees.

They are all about the same age, of course, but measuring them now (as older plants many years later) would erroneously suggest varying ages. Likewise, then, determining the age of the Garland cedar elm can only be an estimate at best. And it does not help that cedar elms are not included in the list of growth factors provided by the International Society of Arboriculture.

Tree-ring counts are also not accommodating in dating cedar elms. Viewed in cross section, cut-down cedar elms reveal very indistinct rings. Even when tree rings can be numbered, they can be misleading. Especially in Texas, various trees might form a growth ring, stall during a protracted dry spell, and then during a better period (that same year) perhaps produce another ring. That would be more than one extraordinarily narrow ring per year, making dating by cross section extremely hard.

And, no, the established growth factor for American elms (4) cannot be used for cedar elms. A glance at the established growth-factor list shows, for instance, that the numbers for oak species deviate significantly (red oak 4, white oak 5, for example). So from a scientific point of view, the Garland homeowner's cedar elm question remains pretty much unanswerable.

Which, naturally, wasn't sufficient for stubborn me to give up on the question.

Cedar Elm Estimate

In part, I couldn't quite quit because we have grown cedar elms from saplings. I can date ours, including a reasonable surmise about their age at the time of purchase. I have observed that their thickening of trunk girth is very slow, particularly in the hot hardscrabble setting that is our backyard.

So my surmise here is hardly scientific. It is anecdotal—meaning based on fallible personal observation and therefore only hypothetical concerning the growth factor for cedar elms. Calculating how many years my cedar elms have been in the ground, including their probable age at the time of purchase, I derived a growth factor of 2.75. I am frankly skeptical about this figure, which strikes me as possibly too low.

However, this is the factor I derived from calculating my trees, and so I suggested that the Garland homeowner try 2.75. She determined that the circumference of her cedar elm was 120 inches. Dividing 120 by 3.14 (pi) yielded a diameter of 38.2 inches. Multiplying 38.2 by my presumed factor of 2.75 resulted in an estimated age of 105 years.

How reliable was this outcome, I wondered. I wished for another coordinate, as it were. Was there something else I could use to reinforce the estimate of 105 years?

Then the homeowner mentioned the age of her home. Built in 1940, her house was seventy-four years old at the time of her question. A photo of her front yard suggested, moreover, that the tree did not appear to have been planted intentionally so close to the house after its construction. Instead, the elm seems to have already been growing in place before the house was built. Apparently its size in 1940 was then taken into consideration when constructing the home.

So from this new perspective, the elm was at least seventy-four years old (the age of the home when I was calculating)—plus enough years (twenty-five to thirty?) for that tree to be sufficiently tall and thick to be taken into account prior to construction.

Assessed now from two angles—both admittedly speculative—the Garland cedar elm appeared to be at least 100 years old, which the homeowner was pleased to hear. Adding "at least" seems necessary. In my opinion, even when using the established growth-factor numbers provided by the International Society of Arboriculture formula, the result for droughty regions is likely a provisional bottom ("at least") number, not the top number for a tree's age. And in the case of the Garland cedar elm, it is altogether likely (particularly if my personally derived cedar-elm growth factor is probably low) that this tree is well over 100 years old.

At least it is "pretty to think so."

✎ 10 ✎

What Does It Take to Raise Standards?

When raising children, establishing standards can be challenging. When raising plants, fortunately, establishing standards is much easier and more fun.

"Standards" are woody shrubs trained to look like little trees. The foliage and flowers of a standard, also known as a patio tree, are allowed to develop only at the top of a long, bare, straight stalk. Sometimes two or three thin stalks can be braided to form a single woven unit.

While vines are the easiest type of plant for fashioning a braided standard, a remarkable number of bushes can be styled into single-stem patio trees. In fact, some of the fun in creating standards is discovering which plants look elegant as small trees.

While forming a standard is far less trouble than dealing with a bonsai or even a topiary, the process takes time. For gardeners without the time or interest in personally designing their own, established patio trees are available at local nurseries and big box stores. But expect to pay a premium for the extra nursery attention already given to these plants. Be prepared to dig even deeper into your pocket to buy a braided standard.

Using Standards

As land values have expanded and the size of new home landscapes has shrunk, patio trees have become increasingly popular. Standards offer striking focal points for courtyards, decks, patios, and balconies.

'Brilliant Pink Iceberg' rose grown as a standard

They can transform a ho-hum doorway, corner, or wall into a "wow" floral showcase.

Because of their tidy appearance, some patio trees can add a touch of formality to a landscape. Whether planted in pots or the ground, their well-groomed vertical features offer a welcome contrast to the bushiness of neighboring plants. Standards can surprise the eye with an unexpected, even unique, perspective on a plant. A rose grown not as a typical bush, but as a seemingly exotic patio tree, commands the viewer to pause for a second look.

Often, too, standards can give an impression of miniaturization, a hint of Lilliputian fantasy. Patio trees sometimes seem to belong in a child-scaled garden or to have been pilfered from Alice's Wonderland.

Creating Standards

Cultivating standards is basically an exercise in strategic pruning. The procedure is simple.

Start with a young woody plant with at least one healthy straight stem. Ideally, this plant should be well established in the ground or a planter. Trim away every stem except one straight stalk (referred to as the "leader"). Clip the other stalks off as close as possible to the plant's roots.

Then insert a sturdy four- to six-foot stake next to the remaining leader stem. At about two-inch intervals, securely fasten the leader to the stake with plastic or cloth ribbons tied in a shoelace bow. These ties will keep the plant straight, but bind the stem loosely to allow for trunk thickening. As the plant grows taller, calculate the leader height that suits you. This is usually between three and five feet, depending on the plant's potential, the stake's length, and your wishes.

The next step determines the maximum height of a patio tree. Cut off the uppermost node. (A node is a stem segment where leaves or buds appear, and the topmost node is where the highest leaves or buds have formed.) Once it is "topped," the leader will not grow any higher.

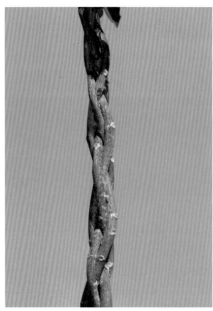

The braided stems of a standard

Safeguard four of the remaining top nodes, but snip off all foliage or buds appearing farther down the cropped leader. The goal is to have the leader branch out only from the four preserved top nodes.

Although a stem braid is sometimes possible, styling it is particularly slow going. A braided standard is fashioned from separate plants or from various different stalks on a single plant. For braided patio trees, follow the procedures for single-stalk standards, but also manually wrap two, three, or four—three is generally considered especially attractive—leaders around each other as the plant grows. With some plants, such as ficus, if the braid is started with very young and pliable stems, the combined stalks will fuse at points to produce a unique visual effect.

Maintaining Standards

Periodically, a patio tree should be gently retied to its stake to accommodate expanding trunk girth. Maintaining a standard also requires cutting away any volunteer (sucker) shoots appearing at the base of the plant. Likewise, all leaves or branches resprouting below the four-node crown must be continually clipped off.

Managing the crown's foliage is a little more demanding. As this preserved foliage crown of the standard begins to fill in and spread, from time to time trim it lightly to foster fullness and roundness. Snipped tips encourage more branching, but each branch should first be allowed to develop several internodal segments before it is shortened.

Leave the hedge sheers in the shed, though. Hard pruning ruins a crown's look by curtailing flowering and fostering unsightly long shoots.

Keeping a patio tree's look requires some attention to proportion, too. A general rule for standards holds that the width of its top foliage ball should measure about one-third of its trunk's length. So a three-foot patio tree usually looks best with a one-foot-wide crown. But this rule is flexible, depending on the plant. In some cases—the 'Grande' firebush (*Hamelia patens*) we grew, for example—a larger than average top does not create an eyesore.

For potted standards, the larger the crown, the greater the risk of tipping over. Since patio trees are sometimes top-heavy and fairly delicate, they are easily tumbled and damaged by wind, children, and pets. Choose large sturdy planters and invest in attractive containers to show off patio trees to advantage.

In Texas, unfortunately, potted plants tend to dry out rapidly from sun, heat, and wind. So the vigor, appearance, and flowering of most of our standards benefit when situated for afternoon shade and when their draining soils are hydrated regularly, as needed.

Winter is another consideration. In-ground standards can be protected by mulching roots and wrapping trunks with pipe insulation. A large trashcan, turned upside down and covered with blankets, helps for smaller in-ground standards.

Potted patio trees, especially tropicals, are particularly vulnerable to winter temperatures in most of Texas. Potted roots are less insulated than in-ground roots. A dolly or, even better, a PotLifter facilitates moving tropicals indoors.

While being overwintered indoors, most standards need bright light from an untinted southern window. They also require much less moisture than when maintained outdoors during summer. Keeping inside standards on the dry side and skipping all feeding will provide for a quicker comeback in the spring. Some, such as hibiscus, slowly shed their leaves during the colder months—ours remain evergreen while wintering indoors beneath plant lights—but they refresh quickly during the following growing season.

Choosing Standards

That potted standards are less cold-hardy than those in the ground should be kept in mind when thinking about which selections to purchase. In fact, even in-ground patio trees are generally less hardy than their shrubby versions. So, to hedge your bet with in-ground choices, you could select cold-hardiness zone 6 plants for planting in zone 7, zone 7 plants for zone 8, and zone 8 plants for zone 9.

Some suitable and easy-to-grow choices for Texas include rosemary, rose of Sharon (*Hibiscus syriacus*), and *Camellia japonica*. Indian hawthorn (*Rhaphiolepis indica*) and roses, including the 'Iceberg' series, also work well. Butterfly bush (*Buddleia davidii*) is available in patio-tree versions, such as 'Black Knight' with wine-hued flowers and 'Harlequin' with variegated leaves.

In-ground selections for Central and South Texas range from oleander (*Nerium oleander*) and Australian bottlebrush (*Callistemon*) to *Euryops pectinatus* 'Viridis.' Each is beautiful but also vulnerable to prolonged freezes.

For planters, there are so many tropical candidates that it's hard to settle on one or even ten. Bougainvillea, hibiscus (*H. rosa-sinensis*), and gardenia (*G. jasminoides*) remain popular choices, among others.

The growing demand for patio trees has led to increasingly surprising standard creations—for instance, 'Inca Sun' brugmansia, blue glory bower (*Clerodendrum ugandense*), honeysuckle fuchsia (*Fuch-*

sia triphylla), and golden dewdrop (*Duranta erecta*). Harder to find and to train as standards, but not to be overlooked, are blue hibiscus (*Alogyne huegelii*) from Australia and Cape mallow (*Anisodontea × hypomandarum*) from South Africa.

For an especially unusual sight—sure to generate conversation—try styling 'Mabel Grey' pelargonium (*Pelargonium citronellum*) into a nearly two-foot standard. Since there is no woody stem in this case, this fragile so-called scented geranium will always need its stake. Several cultivars of *P. crispum* (including 'Lemon Balm,' 'Clorinda,' and 'Purple Unique') offer other trainable pelargonium selections.

It takes at least two years to form a pelargonium standard, and usually it takes even longer to fashion patio trees from other plants. While standards are easy enough to create, they will not be rushed! So the gardener undertaking to raise them from the time they are young should already possess a high personal standard for patience.

11

Where Are My Holly Berries?

Recently another gardener asked, "Where are my holly berries?" A good question, and, in fact, even among botanists, hollies still raise many unanswered questions. We'll get to those in a little bit, but first let's celebrate winter's berried treasures.

For most Texans, winter does not bring totally shorn gardens. We continue to enjoy a wide variety of evergreens (such crossvine, African iris, and lilyturf) as well as, with luck, various other plants we coax through the coldest months. Still, the deciduous plants in our yards defoliate, often leaving our winterscapes barer than we prefer.

That's the case for me whenever my pomegranate bushes go blank after brightening autumn with intense yellow foliage. Unlike some desperate squirrels, I don't particularly value the few dark pomegranates still dangling from wintry leafless branches. Instead, I am on the lookout for plants that enrich my winterscapes with troves of berried treasures.

In describing these plants here, I use the word "berry" loosely, not strictly botanically. Nor does the word "berry" imply edibility. Whereas various birds and other wildlife eat many of the so-called berries mentioned here, most of these fruits are more or less toxic if ingested by us. Children and pets are particularly vulnerable. Such toxicity is hardly unusual, even in ordinary houseplants. Most plants produce foliage, flowers, or fruits containing chemicals designed to deter unwelcome foragers.

Possumhaw (*Ilex decidua*), a small US native holly reaching about fifteen feet, heads my list of winter favorites. Like pomegranate, possumhaw parades yellow leaves in the fall; but after these leaves detach, possumhaw (unlike pomegranate) offers long-lasting red berries look-

Possumhaw

ing like small holiday ornaments abundantly dotting branch-strands.

Also known as winterberry—though not to be confused with common winterberry (*I. verticillata*)—this deciduous holly is not fussy. It excels in a variety of soils, although slightly acidic conditions are especially supportive. Winterberry does fine in a range of sunlight exposures, too, but generally needs about six hours of direct light daily to produce full-berried branches. The berries can last all winter unless raided by songbirds, raccoons, and other rummaging wildlife.

Only female possumhaws bear berries, and so a nearby male plant is required for bees to complete pollination. That may sound like a nuisance, but it isn't because possumhaw, like many other hollies, can easily complete its reproductive cycle with pollen from the male plants of various other holly species.

For winter color, evergreen hollies are a more traditional choice than winterberry. Evergreen hollies are popular because they are hard to beat for visual impact all year. Highly adaptable, drought-tolerant, and deer-resistant Burford holly (*I. cornuta* 'Burfordii') is probably the

'Pride of Houston' yaupon holly

most prominent type in my Texas encounters, though the eye-catching 'Nellie R. Stevens' hybrid also presents a spectacular display. Both enhance our property-wide windbreak along the sidewalk.

Wild hollies dot East Texas, home of the tall American holly (*I. opaca*). However, in *Native Texas Plants* Sally Wasowski advises Houston residents to plant 'Savannah,' a holly hybrid that is "better adapted to clay and won't get algae on its leaves from too much humidity."

Yaupon holly (*I. vomitoria*) is more widespread in our state, where it apparently serves as a potential pollinator for other holly species. Yaupon holly tolerates shade or full-sun exposure as well as dry or moist settings. It can be grown as a bush or a tree, and I have even seen it cultivated as a patio standard (tree-shaped in a pot and requiring periodic pruning that might preclude some berry-bearing). 'Pendula' is a weeping variety of yaupon holly.

Yaupon holly grows slowly and also, in our yard at least, it is far from aggressive. In fact, our understory yaupons have inclined away from "pushy" neighboring plants, such as primrose jasmine (*Jasminum mesnyi*). Even so, ours have withstood everything our neglect and nature have thrown at them, including ice. They are so tough that the yaupons burned during the devastating fire in the Lost Pines forest in Bastrop have quickly resprouted from charred stumps and roots—an ability unfortunately unavailable to the loblolly pines. Since the small luminous red berries of yaupon are long-lasting because they are not significant in any animal's diet, these hollies remain high on my winter-color list.

The arching branches of American beautyberry (*Callicarpa americana*) also score high on my list of winter delights. This understory plant is very companionable, an opportunist that often voluntarily shows up to fill in shady nooks.

American beautyberry is a rangy plant with largish, floppy leaves—hardly a knockout as a stand-alone selection. We let it slowly spread on its own in our drip-irrigated, unlawned windbreak. Various over-wintering birds can't resist this greenbelt's protective shady niches offering a bonus opportunity to feast on magenta beautyberry fruit.

A white-fruited variety (*C. americana* var. *lactea*) is available at nurseries. Known as snowberry, it looks great for a while but tends to lack the winter endurance of the purple-fruited native. Also, unlike the purple berries, the white ones lose their luster and easily become blemished by yellowish-brown spots.

Juvenile mockingbird and American beautyberry

While South Texans might still enjoy the red fruit of pigeonberry (*Rivina humilis*) during winter, gardeners in much of the eastern half of our state can count on coralberry (*Symphoricarpos orbiculatus*). In winter this fast-growing native thicket plant, also known as Indian currant, bears dense clusters of coral or red fruit.

Coralberry can be finicky. In lime or chalky soils it is prone to chlorosis (insufficient chlorophyll due to nutrient deficiencies), and in clay soils it is likewise prone to mildew. Still, in uncrowded settings with good drainage, coralberry can serve as an elevated groundcover.

When cut back substantially, its new arched branches fill in more fully than do those of the less fussy but sprawling American beautyberry. Like beautyberry, though, coralberry spreads easily and so in cultivated beds it too might require intervention.

Western soapberry (*Sapindus drummondii*) is so common across Texas that it could be easily overlooked as a berry choice for winter. This native plant is amazingly adaptable to a variety of draining settings, but its height varies depending on how much rain it receives. It is also, unfortunately, not a long-lived tree.

The leaf pattern of soapberry looks like downsized pecan foliage, but its yellow-to-orange autumnal show is all its own. After its leaves detach, amber berries—large and waxy—ornament the tree during winter. These fruits, incidentally, should not be confused with the softer yellow (and worthless) ones of the notoriously invasive Chinaberry tree (*Melia azedarach*).

Western soapberry fruits, Matt Warnock Turner has explained in *Remarkable Plants of Texas*, "contain up to 37% saponins, which are surfactants (surface-active agents) that reduce surface tension and foam when shaken, as in the case of soap." Although the mashed hydrated berries will clean your hands, Turner has noted, "there are reports of contact dermatitis."

Gardeners in southern half of the state can delight in golden dewdrop (*Duranta erecta*), a Floridian tropical with sky-blue flowers that (as we saw earlier) can also be grown as a patio tree. This duranta yields tear-shaped yellow berries in early fall that have a good chance of lasting into winter. Golden dewdrop attracts butterflies, does well in heat, and thrives in organically rich, draining soils. We position this arching plant near other plants to provide it some shade during summer, and we water it during dry spells.

Farther north in Texas, incidentally, this woody perennial can reach about three feet, die back in winter, and may survive freezes if its roots are protectively mulched. Overwintered containers would be a safer bet.

Four More Berries

Barbados cherry (*Malpighia glabra*), an avian favorite, is a small, freeze-sensitive South Texas evergreen bearing red fruits. These berries make a delicious jelly, though eating them raw is not advised. The fruits can embellish winter if birds have not devoured them by then.

Gardeners in Corpus Christi and the Valley can appreciate the red fruits of desert yaupon (*Schaefferia cuneifolia*), which is as tough as yaupon holly. Its yellow flowers are tiny, like those of agarita; but unlike agarita, its berries have a better chance of still being around to decorate early winter.

A little farther north, shade-loving Oregon grapeholly (*Mahonia aquifolium*), a North American native barberry with spiny leaves, produces yellow flowers in the spring and pale purple-blue fruits by early fall that endure through winter. It is best tucked among other plants in dappled shade with slightly acidic soil. The bird-attracting "grapes" make an excellent preserve.

The hot fruits of chile pequin (*Capsicum annuum*) are technically berries, and I enormously value their contribution to my winterscape. A chile pequin ornamented with tiny red peppers allows me to imagine that something of the past spring and summer has somehow been magically preserved in the heart of winter. The fruits eventually vanish; after all, this easily grown understory native (southward from Waco) is also aptly known as bird pepper.

Overlooked Berries

There are many other plants with berries that we tend to overlook during winter, such as various yews, junipers, and Carolina buckthorn (*Frangula caroliniana*). Another is silverberry (*Elaeagnus pungens*), a thorny Japanese hedge-evergreen that has proved to be Texas-tough in draining settings. Depending on the cultivar, reddish-brown drupes can offer early-winter fare for birds.

A more graceful hedge-shrub, the female wax myrtle (*Morella cerifera*) carries bluish-white berries during winter. This plant can endure heat, drought, and poor drainage.

The white-to-pink flowers of Indian hawthorn (*Rhaphiolepis indica*) form distinctive purple berries in the fall, a welcome ornamental plus that often lasts into winter. A widely popular bush utilized as a border evergreen in draining sites, Indian hawthorn needs plenty of sun and moisture, though not to excess.

And don't overlook our many Texas native sumacs (*Rhus* sp.). Their dense clusters of bird-attracting reddish or whitish drupes, known as sumac bobs, are welcome freebies adorning our winters with sky-high color.

Four Beauties Gone Bad

Some readers might wonder why I skipped easy-to-grow heavenly bamboo (*Nandina domestica*), which so many of us prize for its color-rich foliage and all-winter-long red berries. Regrettably, as reported by Texas AgriLife Extension and also the Lady Bird Johnson Wildflower Center, this nandina has become highly invasive in many parts of our state. Some dwarf cultivars (including 'Gulf Stream' and 'Nana Purpurea') are sterile, while others (such as 'Compacta,' 'Harbour Dwarf,' and 'Firestorm') produce only occasional berries.

Many cultivars of *Ligustrum* were once touted as great landscape choices, too—so much so that they seem to be just about everywhere. Their lasting blue berries add color to winter, but they seed new plants rapidly and possibly surpass nandina as a monoculture threat to Texas native habitats.

For winter color it's hard to beat the striking red, orange, and yellow berries of firethorn (*Pyracantha coccinea*). It's invasive, as well, and also a nasty plant to manage. Its extremely sharp thorns can completely ruin car tires and seriously injure unwary children and pets.

The orange berries of highly adaptable Chinese pistache (*Pistacia chinensis*) brighten winter. Only the female trees of this species, often featuring gorgeous foliage during autumn, bear these distinctive clusters. As I mentioned earlier, pistache seeds germinate easily and have proven to be invasive in some parts of our state.

Missing Holly Berries

Sometimes holly drupe production goes sideways. Hence the question: "Where are my holly berries?" If botanists struggle to answer with certainty, that's because both the extent and the limitations of cross-pollination among hollies are not yet well understood.

Relatively rare leaf-shedding (deciduous) hollies, including possumhaw and common winterberry, are less scientifically documented than the more prominent evergreen hollies, including yaupon. Fred Galle's extensive taxonomic book titled *Hollies* only mentions sketchy "reports of" certain hollies successfully cross-pollinating or failing to cross-pollinate.

So when it comes to using these three Texas native hollies in our landscapes, we are counting on a certain amount of good luck with drupe production by female plants. Most of the time we do quite well because our purchased female hollies get their required pollen from unseen suitable/compatible male holly donors located somewhere else.

Holly Settings

When thinking about native hollies, notice how often the most impressive displays you have seen were plants in open spaces. Although my clustered Burford hollies are annually productive in our windbreak, such crowded plants have less of a chance of being pollinated by some compatible male holly on someone else's property. Location, in short, can be important.

Be sure, too, that hollies are not situated downhill from lawns that are fertilized or (worse yet) treated with pesticides and herbicides. I have seen people accidentally kill foundation plants, including hollies and yews, by failing to notice that heavy rains on treated lawns result in dire chemical impacts on nearby ornamental flora. Too much nitrogen, for instance, will stimulate hollies (and many other plants) into stem- and leaf-production at the cost of flowering/fruiting. This could be a factor for one frustrated grower of berryless mature possumhaws, which are (she complained) sprouting only "new growth all over the place."

Besides location, enticing bees to your hollies helps. Bees are holly pollinators, but bees are hardly plentiful these days, it seems to me.

We'll be discussing this bee situation next, but responding to our specific subject of berry production at this point, aim for substantial companion plantings that attract bees as one way to benefit nearby native hollies.

Dreaded Drought

Prolonged dryness is also a factor, not only in the reduced number of bees but also in the reduced number of holly berries. Drought can cause male blooms and compatible female blooms to emerge at different times rather than at the same time, and this lack of synchronicity would result in little to no pollination.

Drought can cause premature berry drop, though such early, dehydrated fruits are so small that the typical viewer might not notice. Hollies are tough and can withstand long stretches without water, but forcing them to expend their carbohydrates during survival mode will end in little to no berry production. In the wild, Texas hollies tend to prefer thickets along streams, a fact suggesting that these plants are more likely to produce berries with some hydration to ease the effects of extended dry conditions. After all, berries contain a high percentage of water.

Droughts also cause animals—remember the fig-filching skunk?—to forage for the moisture in fruits that they might normally ignore during better times. Sometimes this means that holly berries disappear while unripe and before we get to appreciate them. On the other hand, it is helpful to hollies when birds consume ripe berries later on, thereby opening branch space for next year's flowers. Our neighborhood yaupon berries, which usually continue to look beautifully succulent throughout winter, are often a big attraction for flocks of hungry cedar waxwings during March.

Seasonal bad luck with hollies includes a late freeze that destroys holly blooms or perhaps a heavy population of grasshoppers that devastates the berries. And although you might not catch them doing it, some dogs—including our culpable huskies—don't eat the toxic berries but nonetheless delight in nipping them off one at a time just for fun.

Texas native hollies are highly adaptable as home landscape plants in shrub or tree form. So most of us, thankfully, have trouble-free experiences with them. Even so, I have heard about hollies being a bit persnickety—not as badly as are our huskies, but still . . . Although I have not seen it happen to any of ours, I have learned that some hollies will exhibit a quirky behavior known as "cycling." This refers to periods when some plant function (such as flowering or fruiting) clicks off for a time or skips a year or two for reasons not at all perfectly obvious to us.

Which returns us to my starting point: hollies still raise many unanswered questions. Even so, we'll continue to prize them anyway.

12

Can Dreaded Bolting "Bee" Okay?

Hollies are merely one type of the many plants dependent on bee pollination. Although our honey and native bees are vitally crucial in the natural scheme, something terrible has happened to these workaholics during the last decade or so.

In most of our nation, including Texas, honeybees have contracted known and unknown viral infections, resulting in compromised immune systems and collapsed colonies. Although Israeli acute paralysis virus has been identified as one contributory culprit, exactly what accounts for the extent of today's bee-colony collapse remains uncertain. Environmental changes, various diseases, pesticides, and monocultural agriculture are being studied as possible culprits. Whatever the cause, scientists, farmers, and gardeners alike are concerned about the consequences.

With beekeepers reporting a sudden and substantial loss of colonies, farmers who depend on bees to pollinate their plants have struggled to maintain their livelihood. Such "pollinator decline," reads a recent report by the National Research Council, has the "potential to alter the shape and structure of the terrestrial world."

That's chillingly clear enough. Just think how much of what we count on in our world depends upon bees, from agricultural produce to our beloved wildflowers.

Bee Specifics

There are many kinds of bees, including hundreds of understudied species in Texas. Some feed only on a single plant species. Some have floral preferences but will adapt in a pinch. Others are perfectly content with almost any flower offering nectar easily lapped up by tiny apian tongues. One nondiscriminator, the European honeybee (*Apis mellifera*), is particularly important to agriculture, even though its various varieties are technically invasive exotics and are susceptible to hazardous crossbreeding with African honeybees.

A fresh colony of honeybees is formed when a newly mated queen swarms—that is, leaves her birth hive with many worker bees. The drones (males) in her party usually die before winter. The sterile female workers last longer. The queen, if not subjected to a hive upset, will live between three and five years.

Bees were once wasps that changed their ways millions of years ago, sometime after the appearance of the first flowers. I imagine they found that nectar tasted better than fellow insects.

Bee Smarts

Honeybees have developed a dance-language to signal each other about the location of certain flowers. A circular dance reports short distances, while a figure-eight dance refers to distances of over a hundred yards. Each spring honeybees remember where to find last year's nectar-rich flowers. They identify their proper hive by its unique scent.

Bumblebees (*Bombus* sp.)—recognized by their yellow-banded, fuzzy black bodies—don't dance. They have learned a different trick called "buzz pollination." When visiting a flower they change the pitch of their buzz until pollen grains are vibrated out of a flower's anthers.

The expression "worker bee" is no exaggeration. Some bees start at the bottom of a stem and proceed upward in an efficient spiral pattern from flower to flower. They repeat this pattern over and over. It takes visits to about 9 million flowers—that's over 7,000 bee-hours—to produce one pound of honey, which is a distillation of bee-snatched nectar.

Bee Support

Gardeners cannot fix whatever is happening to our precious pollinators, but they can create bee-supportive habitats. The good news is that native bees are capable of doing a considerable amount of the work usually performed by honeybees. The bad news is that these native bees have also declined.

A bee-supportive habitat should be pesticide-free. Its size should be larger rather than smaller, offering a wide number and variety of flowers available from spring through autumn.

Native plants are particularly helpful. However, bees will raid many nonnative flowers—for example, the multihued garden "escapes" of *Lantana camara.* They put to good use the purplish blooms of devil's trumpet (*Datura metel*), bluebeard (*Caryopteris*), and rose of Sharon (*Hibiscus syriacus*), among many other plants that are popular in Texas gardens.

Bees often reject the alkaloid nectars of the heath family (*Ericaceae*), but it remains unsettled as to precisely which plants are rejected by which bees. Ericaceous blueberries, for instance, are specifically pollinated by native bees. On the other hand, there are unconfirmed reports that the alkaloid nectar of the widely planted, yellow-trumpeted Carolina jessamine (*Gelsemium sempervirens*) is toxic to bees.

Bolting

Since the destruction of natural habitats has likely contributed to native bee and honeybee decline, an apian-friendly garden might help to make a difference—might just "bee" in time to help. And such a garden could include flowering herbs. Although some specialty chefs are experimenting with edible herbal blooms, gardeners generally don't want their herbs to flower. Bees, however, love it when they do.

By late February Catherine and I usually have purchased a number of culinary herbs. We grow them in containers, sometimes closely companioned with small ornamentals such as begonias, marigolds, and creeping Jenny. In addition, we have a large and wide-spreading bush of prolifically blooming in-ground Mexican oregano that has thrived for many years in our unlawned windbreak.

We choose these herbs sometimes for culinary purposes but more often just for their look, scent, and bee support. Unlike most people

Mexican oregano

who grow herbs for kitchen use, we do not much care if or when ours bloom.

Even so, I have been curious about the different timing of our herbs' flowering. Our Italian oregano, for instance, tends to bloom by late spring, while our nearby beautiful Greek oregano goes flowerless for much longer and our 'Hot & Spicy' oregano never blossoms. Then there is our potted Thai basil, which is usually located next to the oreganos, yet flowers prematurely (bolts) within a few days after being transplanted into a container.

So, for me, questions about bees easily morphs into questions about bolting.

In horticulture, the word "bolt" refers to the unwelcome production of flowering parts—*unwelcome* because blooms reduce the harvesting-value of the plants. Such premature flowering diverts plant resources away from valued edible parts (such as foliage and roots), resulting in less produce and also usually poorer-quality produce. As it devotes nearly all its resources to flower and seed production even at the cost of its own life, a fully bolted plant bears fewer, less tender leaves that also tend to be less tasty, perhaps even bitter.

Gardeners do not care if their ornamentals flower early—the earlier and the longer, in fact, the better. They don't care if, while flowering, ornamental-plant foliage becomes tough and bitter to the taste of foraging animals. We do care, however, if we are growing greens we want to eat.

Some veggies are particularly prone to bolt, including the basils we buy each year. Spinach, broccoli, cilantro, and onions, among some other veggies, are quick bolters, too. Possibly, lettuce is the most bolt-prone crop we can try to grow in sun-drenched Texas. And if you ever sampled a leaf from a lettuce head adorned with a flower stalk, you won't likely repeat that unsavory mistake.

Causes and Effects

A culinary plant flowers prematurely when its environment sets off genetic codes signaling the plant to "finish up." Then various hormones are triggered that create a fast track to reproduction through flower and seed formation. With its mission nearly accomplished, the individual plant hardly matters at this point; what matters is survival of the species through each dying plant's seed dispersal. Even so, to protect the fading plant a little longer during this species-directed seed stage, bitter chemicals (often starting with vinegary acetic acid) form in both leaves and (increasingly elongated) stems. These chemicals ward off insect and larger animal foragers, including us.

Environmental triggers can vary from one plant species to another. But one prominent factor can be temperature. Cold snaps can cause autumn crops, especially the brassicas, to prematurely flower. Hot weather can affect spring plantings when atmospheric heat eventually warms up the ground, too. Such increased soil temperature is detrimental to any plants (including many herbs) with roots accustomed to cooler settings. The roots of these plants register the threatening rise in ground temperature and signal the rest of the plant to change course from vegetative growth to flower and seed development.

Scientific studies of lettuce reveal that heat is only one factor behind bolting. A second and more important factor is accumulation of light exposure (photoperiodism). An experiment in 1995 revealed that lettuce grown in 90 degrees but restricted to only eight hours of sunlight grew to harvest stage without bolting. Further experiments showed that the overall amount of light exposure mattered more, actually, than heat did in activating premature flowering in lettuce.

Lettuce, like most of our other leafy edible greens, is genetically programmed as a "long-day plant." Long-day plants require a certain total accumulation of light exposure before flowering. They typically flower during the long days of summer and produce seed during autumn. This basic pattern, however, is disrupted if these plants have already accumulated more light during our Texan spring than they would have in their native climates. When this happens, it's as if the plants are already (in a sense) "filled to the brim" with all the light they can possibly process. As we will see, this is an important piece of information for the savvy greens-grower to consider.

So light exposure and heat—two phenomena Texan gardeners know well—are the main culprits behind premature flowering and subsequent flavor loss in our culinary greens. Other factors can come into play as well. Stress from insufficient water or a mineral deficiency has been shown to activate bolting. So can plant crowding. So can low temperatures at early stages during broccoli and other brassica development, for example. And the seemingly simple act of transplanting—as possibly my Thai basils demonstrate—can foster the dreaded onset of bolting.

Bolting Intervention

For most of us in Texas, preventing the bolting of long-day greens is an issue because they tend to behave like short-day plants as our days lengthen. Few of us grow many actual short-day plants (such as rice and certain chrysanthemums), which flower when they don't accumulate enough time in light. And flowering is welcome in many of our day-neutral plants, such as tomatoes and cucumbers, which (thankfully) have no shutdown chemistry in response to too much or too little light. And we don't care at all if the flowering of our tomato plants, for instance, releases bitter chemicals within their pungent foliage.

It is impossible for gardeners to counteract their greens' long-day genetic program. Once a green maxes out on its genetically acceptable amount of light, it starts to flower and shut down for good. But we can fiddle a bit with the environment of these greens to delay their genetic program's various triggers.

Timing is important. Start spring greens as early as possible while days are shorter and the weather is cooler. Start autumn greens as late as possible. It helps to consult updated planting guidelines for Texas. Experimentation with different selections or cultivars of the same green is also useful because not all varieties of the same veggie are equally prone to quick bolting—as is evident with the apparent bolt-resistance of my 'Hot & Spicy' oreganos.

Periodically covering greens with shade cloth also helps reduce total light exposure, but it might be easier to simply position herbs in locations receiving partial sunlight or very bright shade. Mulching greens also can retard bolting because it helps soil to retain moisture and remain cooler.

When my basils start to bolt, I cut off the flower stalks as soon as I spot them. This does not stop the plants from trying to bolt again and again, but it interferes with the process enough for these plants to continue to produce pretty and edible foliage. Unfortunately, not all greens respond this well to flower-stalk lopping.

The Joy of Bolting

So I am no Hamlet of indecision about herb bolting. For me "to bolt or not to bolt" is hardly "the question." I revel in the joy of bolting—for the bees' sake. Bees love most herb flowers, especially the medicinal (*officinalis*) types, which (some beekeepers are persuaded) specifically foster apian health. Possibly, it has been suggested, herb pollen enables bees to withstand the impact of mites, among other benefits. If true, this would be significant because the sucking varroa mite, in particular, has severely affected beekeeping in the United States since this pest's arrival here during the late 1980s. While some beekeepers strongly believe in herbal contributions to the well-being of their apian colonies, the science behind their health claims remains insufficiently established as of yet. On the other hand, recent research has shown that the nectar of native mints (*Monarda* sp.) is indeed bee balm because it demonstrably helps bumblebees ward off internal parasites.

Whatever the science behind the appeal, there is ample evidence that bees flock to herb flowers. At our home bees are particularly attracted to flowering thyme, rosemary, sage, and mint, among other greens. These are all easy to grow, though (*bee* aware!) mints can spread like a wildfire. While bees crave the lavender blooms of the Mexican oreganos in our windbreak, they seem less interested in the tiny white flowers of our Italian oregano, perhaps keeping them in reserve, as needed. Although some lists include basils, especially sacred basil (*Ocimum tenuiflorum*; *O. sanctum*), as a bee magnet, I have never seen a bee on my various basil flowers, which is why I don't feel the least bit selfish when snipping flower stalks to keep this herb as long as possible for my own benefit.

13

How Did Our Bees Get So Blue?

When at some point in natural history bees took notice of flowers, flowers in turn responded to apian attention by advertising nectar. Nectar is a costly process for a plant because it requires the movement of life-sustaining nutrients away from green leaves to flowers, where it serves little purpose other than to attract pollinators.

Like peacock feathers, flowers are an extravagance. The earliest plants, including ferns and gymnosperms, did perfectly fine without any flowers. They did fine, as well, without animals, including us.

It is understandable, however, that people long ago leapt to faulty conclusions about these flowerless plants. It was easy for them to surmise, on the basis of untutored observation, that seed-producing flora must have always dominated the plant realm and that the non-seeders, including ferns and mosses, were either odd deviations from the norm or secret seeders.

When impression-nurtured beliefs are unchecked by science, mischief can ensue. Consider the sixteenth-century notion that ferns actually *do* produce seed because (it was believed) all plants *must* grow from seed. Never mind that no one could see any fern seed or guess the reproductive function of the spore-stuffed sporangia clusters (sori) on the undersides of mature fern fronds. There were answers for these shortcomings, including a legend about what had once happened to fern flowers. According to this ancient legend, ferns did not contribute any blooms at the Christ child's manger. As a punishment for such "bad-seed" irreverence, ferns were henceforth deprived of their flowers and subsequently their seed became invisible.

Autumn fern (Dryopteris erythrosora)

This curse notwithstanding, ferns were still thought long ago to be valuable for various medicinal remedies, and their now-invisible seed was especially prized by the gullible. Some even believed that fern seed could make a person undetectable. Of course, collecting the invisible fern seed was deucedly difficult.

In *An Orchard Invisible,* Jonathan Silvertown doesn't mention the fern flower legend, but he succinctly explains how this imaginary invisible fern seed was harvested: "Fern seed could be collected on the stroke of midnight on Midsummer Night's eve, but only by catching it as it fell from the plant onto a stack of twelve pewter plates. It would pass through the first eleven, but be trapped by the twelfth."

A screwball belief, indeed! But I have been around a while and have seen too much, and so I can't help but wonder whether, even today, empty seed packets labeled "Rare Invisible Fern Seed" might sell pretty well.

Flower Power

Ferns and other seedless plants once ruled our planet's oceans and lands, and the "magic trick" of encapsulating sea-like nutrients inside a seed emerged at some later point in time. Perhaps, at first, some plants were cross- or self-pollinated by wind and water, while others reproduced in a variety of asexual ways. This early history, insofar as it has been unearthed, is entertainingly documented and illustrated in *Fossil Plants* by Paul Kenrick and Paul Davis. Apparently, "flowering plants are comparative newcomers," and the earliest known blooms were small and unimpressive.

The oldest fossil of a *flowering* plant was reported in 2011. This tiny buttercup relative died around 125 million years ago. At present we still know very little about this or any of the other earliest flowering plants, including the million-year-old examples preserved in amber.

There is much to ponder. One intriguing issue is that flowering plants (angiosperms) seem to appear somewhat abruptly in our fragmented fossil records—a fact Charles Darwin once referred to (in an 1879 letter to Joseph Dalton Hooker) as "an abominable mystery." Another and equally intriguing issue relates to the daunting complexity of and variation in floral designs. And still another issue concerns why plants ever produced blooms, given how extravagantly costly (in terms of resources) flowers are for a plant. As we noticed when thinking about bolting herbs, some plants will even deplete themselves to death, if necessary, to produce a single bloom.

Flowering plants eventually dominated our planet and changed it, too. For these plants there must have been a species cost-benefit. Specifically, flowers evidently enhanced their species' prospects for spreading (reproduction). They didn't do this alone, of course. Flowering plants pulled off their worldwide rise to prominence with the help of pollen-dispersing wind and (most especially) the contemporaneous rise of insects that could be enticed by various floral structures, markings, fragrances, nectars, pollens, and colors. Eventually other animals, especially birds and even humans, would figure in this mutually beneficial and complex network.

Bee Vision

The emergence of floral colors is no less curious than the first appearance of flowers. Whereas butterflies possess more acute color vision than bees, birds respond to the visible spectrum even better than butterflies. Birds are highly sensitive to orange-to-red wavelengths. Such wide appeal to both avian and insect pollinators explains the

Texas native thelesperma

predominance of red, orange, and especially yellow blooms among wildflowers.

Many Texas wildflowers belong to the widespread sunflower family, a bee favorite. When bees zero in on yellow flowers, they tend to perceive these blooms as blue to purple. Bees are particularly drawn to yellow flowers with darkly contrasting throats or buttons, such as coreopsis or thelesperma.

White flowers, including the apian favorite buckwheat, also look bluish to bees. White flowers often exhibit bee-attracting features, usually at their centers. In white flowers, yellow often tends to highlight the throats and particularly the reproductive organs (the stigma of the pistil and the anthers of the stamens). We see this pattern, for example, in white blooms of evergreen sumac (*Rhus virens*), prickly poppy (*Argemone albiflora*), spider lily (*Hymenocallis liriosme*), and fragrant water lily (*Nymphaea odorata*).

Which raises a question about bird-luring red flowers. It's been said that since bees are generally not sensitive to the red wavelengths, they rarely visit red flowers.

But you've seen bees visiting pink and red flowers, right? You can find them busily buzzing around the pink blooms of Texas rockroses (*Pavonia lasiopetala*), though these blooms probably appear as bluish to bees. At the edge of our unlawned windbreak I have also seen really early bees plundering red, pink, and orangey-red flowering quince blooms. Quince flowers likely possess bee-directing nectar guides. Even if there were no guides, I suppose a hard-luck bee can't be too choosy in late winter, when there are fewer flowers to raid.

So some enterprising bees utilize flowers that appear to be white, yellow, orange, or red to us. However, bees don't see these colors. Bee vision is designed to benefit from the ultraviolet end of the spectrum. They respond to floral ultraviolet petal patterns (invisible to us) that serve as bluish signposts to bees, which also put to good use such dark-hued nectar guides as "landing-strip" streaks or hairy tufts on flower petals. Flowers that seem uniformly colored to us can, in the polarized vision of bees, register as vibrantly patterned. We can't detect these visual cues any more than bees can appreciate our way of perceiving white, yellow, orange, or red.

Seeing Blue

Since the polarized vision of bees is designed to benefit from the long wavelengths of the blue-to-ultraviolet bands of the spectrum, bees are particularly drawn to purple flowers. For example, in late summer to early autumn they flock to the flashy violet floral "pineapples" of Texas native eryngiums. As early as February in our yard, they plunder the cute lavender-to-purple blooms of henbit (*Lamium amplexicaule*), considered a stressed-lawn nuisance. And the pale blue or the lavender flowers of our rosemary, which also often blooms during February, are likewise native-bee magnets.

Sometimes bees will wait for flowers to change to shades of purple (the floral hue in nature most prevalent after yellow and red). For instance, bees plunder cup-and-saucer vine (*Cobaea scandens*) after its white flowers turn blue. Bees seek out blue even more than purple.

That's why bees flock to a blue-flowered delphinium, agapanthus, roundleaf chastetree (*Vitex rotundifolia*), or Cape plumbago (*P. auriculata*), among other examples. Planting bluebonnets (*Lupinus* sp.), mealy sage (*Salvia farinacea*), and other like-colored wildflowers can convert feeling blue about bee decline into a more hopeful *Rhapsody in Blue*.

While the primary color blue is commonplace in paintings and home decor, in flowers it is a strange and rare deviation from the norm. That may be hard to believe on a summer walk past dappled slopes of weedy dayflowers (*Commelina* sp.). Sprawling dayflowers may seem barely worthy of notice, but in fact their tiny true-blue flowers represent a botanic oddity and deserve a closer look.

The anomaly of blue flowers has become both a fascinating and frustrating brainteaser for botanists. "When I speak to my chemical colleagues about the difficulties for organisms in producing blue colors," biology professor David Lee wrote in *Nature's Palette*, "they express puzzlement." They often can identify a variety of blue pigments, he added, but uncomfortably they also find, when trying to explain blue flowers, that "a clever chemist is not the same as the template of biodiversity and the process of natural selection."

True floral blueness, it turns out, is not the result of one or even two basic mechanisms. Instead, various plant species have developed a variety of singular ways for producing blue flowers.

Blue Carnation and Blue Rose

The complexities behind floral blue have some plant geneticists singing the blues. They haven't found it easy to cash in on the potentially lucrative market for blue flowers. Blue flowers are especially popular in the multibillion-dollar cut-flower trade, which is presently limited to only a few blue floral species, such as irises. That's why some researchers have been trying to genetically customize plants presently lacking that color. It's been a tough struggle with limited results.

In 1996, Florigene, an innovative biotech company in Melbourne, Australia, marketed 'Moondust,' a true-blue carnation. After years of development, this biotechnical novelty became the world's first commercial genetically modified flower. 'Moondust,' which is sterile and so not an environmental threat, was followed by several other blue-carnation cultivars.

With their carnations selling well worldwide, Florigene's scientists intensified their search for the grail of cut flowers—a true-blue rose. The prospect of a unique blue rose has stirred gardeners' imaginations since at least the mid-nineteenth century. It could be said to be a flower to die for, and unsurprisingly it became the subject of a murder-mystery by Anthony Eglin.

Although today there are so-called blue roses, they can be disappointing. These multicrossed hybrids, such as 'Blue Moon' and 'Moon Shadow,' possess no blue pigment and are better described as mauve-lavender in color.

After nearly two decades of trial and error, Florigene announced that it had succeeded in genetically engineering a blue rose. But have they? "It's mauve, not blue," complained Lorraine d'Anda, editor of the Los Angeles Rose Society bulletin. She has a point. Sadly, it is hard to see a significant color difference between today's bluish-lavender hybrid roses and Florigene's blue rose.

The Trouble with Blue

Although the color of the Florigene rose stirs skepticism, the company's researchers have in fact accomplished quite a feat at the genetic level. First they successfully transferred a cloned delphinidin gene from blue petunias to carnations; then they transferred a cloned delphinidin gene from blue pansies to roses. These were important steps because carnations and roses lack delphinidin, which is a synthesizing enzyme enabling the expression of floral blueness.

The Florigene rose, however, also required a facilitating blue enzyme borrowed from iris. And it also needed a lab-created silencing gene to switch off the rose's natural red enzyme, which interferes with the color pathway to blue.

It is very hard to alter the red pathway in plants. This pathway is produced by various other anthocyanins generally more dominant than delphinidin. Besides being the main source for most floral and fruit hues, these other anthocyanins (especially the orange, red, and purple pigments) are crucial to a plant's survival in a variety of ways, including protection from sunburn.

So trying to intervene in the red pathway to enable the expression of blueness is very tricky—and not just for genetic engineers. It's tricky for plants, too. That's why various blue-flowered plants have developed differing, complex, and often unique mechanisms for checking or altering anthocyanin pigments.

Blue-Flower Secrets

Many gardeners already know one chemical "trick" for getting blue instead of pink blooms on bigleaf hydrangeas (*H. macrophylla*). They add aluminum sulfate. The delphinidin in these hydrangeas bonds with the aluminum, which becomes more available in acidic (lower pH) than in alkaline (higher pH) soils. So soil acidity (increased by the sulfate) also significantly contributes to the production of blue hydrangea blooms.

Before applying aluminum sulfate, however, keep in mind that this compound is harmful to some plants, including acid-loving ones (such as rhododendrons and azaleas). Also, many hydrangea species never turn blue. While bigleaf and mountain (*H. serrata*) hydrangeas are particularly celebrated for their blue blooms, sometimes cultivars of these same species lack the necessary pigments and co-pigments. They tend to bear colorless flowers.

If only blueness could be triggered so easily in other flowers! Wishes aside, the hard fact remains that floral blueness depends on barely understood biochemical factors and interactions.

Common dayflower

For example, those seemingly simple dayflowers along the road-side (mentioned earlier) perform a special magic trick by utilizing a charged magnesium atom to express their blue pigment. And true-blue morning glories express their gorgeous color by producing special petal cells with reduced acidity.

As we know from hydrangeas, acidity level is often a major factor in blocking or enabling the blue pathway. To express blueness, some plants need more acidity, others less—either overall or primarily in a petal's surface layer. Unfortunately, changing acidity can easily ruin flowers. Petal acidity, in fact, is one reason why the Florigene rose, despite its engineered possession of 100 percent blue genes, doesn't quite pass the vision test—it doesn't look pansy- or viola- or iris-blue.

True-blue morning glories

So Why So Blue?

Which brings us to a puzzling question: why have some plants developed such elaborate ways to produce blue flowers? The short answer probably is: to attract specific pollinators.

Actually that answer is too short. There are at least two problems with it. First, all floral colors have likely emerged as pollinator attractors. And, second, most pollinators respond to the yellow-to-red end of the spectrum—a good explanation of why blue flowers are statistically rare in nature.

So why bother with blue? The answer seems to be this: to attract bees, those extraordinarily effective and efficient pollinators that not only prefer blue to any other color but also can't resist that color.

While bees are the primary pollinators of blue flowers, sometimes other creatures crash the nectar party. This happens with blue-flowered sages, for instance. I once saw a hummingbird pumping prairie sages (*Salvia azurea*), a Texas native plant. Hummers are also reported to raid anise-scented sages (*S. guaranitica*), a true-blue South American plant that does well in Texas gardens. And while the blue flowers of caryopteris (also known as bluebeard or blue mist) attract bees, their scent also appeals to butterflies.

As the cut-flower industry proves, people crave blue flowers as much as bees do. So it is easy to appreciate the sense of wonder expressed in the opening lines of a haiku by Amy Lowell: "Again the larkspur, / Heavenly blue in my garden."

14

Why Are There Black and Green Flowers?

True blue, as we have seen, is the hardest floral hue for any plant to produce. There are two others that are easier for plants to express but are nonetheless uncommon and can strike us as peculiar: seemingly black and obviously green flowers.

The Black Rose—a book title that stirs the imagination. While Thomas Costain's 1945 bestselling historical romance is actually far tamer than my childhood memory of its earliest paperback cover, its title promises an enticing concoction of exoticness and passion. The "black rose" in that book is a beautiful woman from the medieval East. A leading woman also figures in *The Black Tulip*, Alexandre Dumas's now forgotten 1850s historical novel, which at least mixes romantic infatuation with a quest for the most exotic of flowers during the seventeenth-century Dutch tulip craze.

As these book titles suggest, black-looking flowers inhabit a class of their own. At once strange and desired, atypical and elegant, they command attention. It's hardly surprising, then, that so-called black plants have become a horticultural phenomenon.

Truly Black?

How do some flowers appear to be black? The impression of blackness in plants, biology professor David Lee has explained in *Nature's Palette*, results from oxidation, variations in acidity, odd cell shapes, tannin, and particularly unusual molecular concentrations. These features can combine pigments in ways that absorb the spectral bands more inclusively and more evenly than are typical for most flowers or leaves.

It might help here to briefly observe the floral variations of Confederate rose (*Hibiscus mutabilis*) and the common white-flowered rain lily (*Zephyranthes* sp.). Confederate rose is not considered a black plant, nor (despite its popular name) is it a rose or an Old South native. But this heirloom perennial, so familiar to Texans, offers a lesson about the nature of black flowers. As its species name *mutabilis* indicates, this plant's flowers tend to "mutate" in color. Not all Confederate roses bear flowers that dramatically change their hue, but those that do so open white or pale pink. Then within one to three days they sequence from pink to rose until they turn deep purple-blue before closing. A similar pattern occurs in common white-flowered rain lilies, which pop up overnight in lawns a day or so after a storm and then shortly thereafter fatigue to a rosy pink. Changes in petal-cell acidity levels account for this shift in floral hue in both these plants—a dramatic example of how acidity concentrations also play a role in determining the darkness of seemingly black flowers.

And it is, disappointingly, just a matter of *seemingly* black. The impression of floral blackness is only an optical illusion. "It is impossible to create a truly black flower," Hans Kapiteyn has stated. As a Dutch

Confederate rose (Hibiscus mutabilis 'Rubra')

bulb merchant, Kapiteyn should know. He spent sixteen years breeding and introducing a blackish hyacinth named 'Midnight Mystique.'

It isn't hard to understand Kapiteyn's point. The floral hues we see are those spectral bands (wavelengths) that get reflected back to our eyes because they are not absorbed by the petals. A yellow rose, in other words, absorbs all the bands of visible light except yellow, which is the reflected color we see. Studied closely in bright light, a black-seeming flower (such as a 'Queen of the Night' tulip or Kapiteyn's 'Midnight Mystique' hyacinth) usually reveals faint red-to-purple highlights. That's the case, as well, with *Alcea rosea* 'Nigra,' a hollyhock I once grew. At its best, its flowers appeared to be velvety black, yet often in very bright sunlight its variable blooms revealed an underlying rosy-maroon tinge.

Similar to the darkest floral stage of Confederate rose, black flowers always still express the dominant red pathway. What appears to be black is actually an extreme and uncommon manifestation of red. Which raises a hard question: why have some plants pushed the red

Hollyhock (Alcea rosea "Nigra")

Chapter 14

pathway so far that their flowers appear to be black? Do these flowers in some unique way appeal to pollinators oriented toward ultraviolet wavelengths? So far, the precise function of blackish blooms remains unclear. And the fact that black flowers are rare in nature only deepens the mystery.

Designing in Black

If so-called black flowers are rare in nature, they are not uncommon among plant breeders. In fact, plants with black flowers or foliage have become extremely fashionable.

They are more than fashionable, according to Karen Platt in *Black Magic and Purple Passion*. Black plants, she has stated, have "transcended fashion to become a permanent part of the garden, just as black is a permanent part of most women's wardrobes these days." As a former owner of a black-plants nursery and as the founder of the International Black Plant Society, Platt enjoys an insider's take on positioning solitaire or companioned black plants for eye-popping landscape effects. "Experiment," she counsels. According to Platt, "the ultimate key to the success of a dark garden is the selection of plants with regard to tone, foliage, texture and form."

Or think of designing with them as artwork, Paul Bonine has urged in *Black Plants*. "Even an ordinary garden can be transformed by dark foliage and flowers into a canvas with the depth and play of light and shadow as detailed as a painting by a Dutch realist." Except that, thankfully, designing with black plants isn't as challenging as imitating a Dutch master.

The main fact to keep in mind about including black plants is their considerable power to draw the eye and steal the show. As a result, their bold effect often tends to suit larger settings better than smaller ones. Of course, container compositions are an exception to this advice. Some potted black plants, including the hard-to-believe tropical bat flower (*Tacca chantrieri*) from China, will elicit involuntary oohs and ahs from visitors.

Black Plants for Texas

When it comes to design, perhaps the most challenging matter is the placement of nearly solid-hued blackish plants, particularly if they are as large as purple-black cannas and elephant ears (*Colocasia esculenta*) or as imposing as *Yucca filamentosa* 'Bronze Age' (which turns from green to purple to "black" in cold weather). Such plants can be used for high-impact contrast with other large plants sporting bright-colored blooms.

Smaller plants with dark foliage or flowers, such as the 'Onyx Odyssey' cultivar of *Helleborus* (Lenten rose), which is suitable for North Texas, can be positioned among pastel-hued neighbors to create a more elegant effect. Sometimes, too, blackish plants can be played off each other when their patterns, textures, and sizes vary. So, for example, a coral bells (*Heuchera*) combination of 'Black Beauty,' 'Midnight Rose,' and 'Cowardly Lion' offers fascinating variations on the theme of black. *Actaea* 'Black Negligee' (baneberry) is a possibility for East Texas.

It might be easiest to design with variegated black plants, which provide their own mixed palette. As 'Eclipse' coleus, 'Iron Cross' begonia, 'Happy Violet' pelargonium, and 'Cascade Creeper' tiarella demonstrate, green and black patterns can be quite striking. Bright yellow or chartreuse highlights define *Alocasia* 'Polly,' *Heuchera* 'Cowardly Lion,' and various variegated pelargoniums. For a "louder" effect there are plants that blend black with pink or reddish brown, such as copper plant (*Acalypha wilkesiana*) and 'Tilt-a-Whirl' coleus.

'Iron Cross' begonia

Perhaps it's too unimaginative to mention blackberries and egg-plants, which can get dark enough to appear black. Also, there are black cherry tomatoes. But 'Black Pearl' peppers are something else altogether. These peppers look so dark and sleek that they seem utterly unreal. They always demand a second look, and even then it's hard to believe they are not a black-magic optical illusion.

Green Flowers

Green flowers are far more common in nature than "black" flowers. Nevertheless, in a world dominated by red and yellow flowers, green ones can seem strange. Possibly the flashy greenies promoted by nurseries can seem peculiar largely because green flowers in the wild tend to be small and so go unnoticed.

"It's not that easy being green," Kermit the Frog sings, "Having to spend each day the color of the leaves / When I think it could be nicer being red, or yellow or gold." Unlike Kermit, flowers should find it "comfortable" to be green. Surprisingly, however, most flowers are not green, and this odd fact gives the greenies a special garden cachet. Green flowers seem so unusual that they are treated as pricey gardening exotics.

Shouldn't green flowers be common? Shouldn't green be not only the easiest color for plants to produce florally but also the best option for maximizing even more life-sustaining, chlorophyll-generated carbohydrates?

Botanists, as we noted earlier, theorize that the rise of flowers co-incided with the rise of insect populations. I am sure they are right. Enhanced insect assistance in reproduction indeed seems to be a principal factor in the emergence of flowers.

I have often wondered, however, whether floral hues (other than green) were also meant to distract insects away from precious life-sus-taining leaf-factories. If my surmise has any merit, then potential leaf-chomping nuisances could be enticed away from long-term leaves to alluring short-term flowers, where these redirected critters might be converted into inadvertent pollinators. After all, nectar is much sweet-er than leaf-juice—I once found that out for myself as a preschooler sampling some hedge foliage and also some honeysuckle flowers. Since blooms are disposable, marauding-insect damage to them (rather than to leaves) would matter little to the survival of an individual plant.

Perhaps flowers became a cost-effective, expendable resource first and foremost to protect life-critical foliage and simultaneously served to attract pollinators to propagate various plant species.

Just Modified Leaves

The beauty of flowers hardly escapes our notice. On the other hand, their appealing intricacy and variation tend to blind us to the most commonly unrecognized fact about flowers: they are modified leaves, which are green.

Sepals are the modified leaves that usually protect a bud and then sometimes serve as the outer whorl of a bloom. The corolla of petals within these sepals is another form of leaf modification. The floral tepals of tulips are neither sepals nor petals, but still another variation on modified leaves.

While petals are celebrated for their wondrous display of colors, sepals can also contribute striking hue and form to a flower. That's the case with most orchids with a dorsal and two lateral sepals looking like petals. Brightly tinted bracts (modified foliage distinct from the flower) can also look like petals. Bracts, not petals, give eryngo its intense purple luster and also give poinsettia its luscious red velvety appearance.

My point is that sometimes we have to look very closely at a flower to spot which forms of modified foliage account for its colorful impact. But whether floral showiness is the result of petals, sepals, tepals, or bracts, in every instance their underlying genetic code expresses protein mutations on the theme of "leaf."

And this genetic predisposition explains why green flowers are not in the least mysterious. They simply display the chlorophyll pigment of their leafy origin. Chlorophyll is a superabundant resource for a life-form that thrives primarily by photosynthesis. Chlorophyll molecules absorb all of the waves of light except green (the "reflected" foliage hue we see). Such sunlight-absorbance maximizes the energy-capture capacity of leaves. As modified leaves, then, flowers should find it resourceful to be green.

Yet, as we have seen, most flowering plants have developed complex chemical processes for producing colors other than green. So the real mystery with green flowers is the degree to which they are downplayed in nature.

Shades of Green

The unearthed vestiges of the earliest flowers don't reveal their color, but I'd bet that they came in shades of green and did not seem especially appealing to insects. I'm just guessing, of course. However it was then, flowers eventually paraded other colors to attract pollinators, though color is only one motivator. Floral shape, odor, and ultraviolet patterns frequently play a role, too, and so many green flowers likely attract insects by means other than color.

Because of their unusualness in the garden, green flowers have given rise to a growing number of devotees. Alison Hoblyn, author of *Green Flowers*, appreciates their "humility," like "a kind of comma, somewhere to rest the eye between stimulating and opposing coloured areas." When green flowers are planted together, Hoblyn suggests, they give us "an opportunity not to be distracted by showy hues and instead look hard at the form of the plant."

She could also have mentioned the subtle beauty we find in various shades of green. Green is not a uniform color. In many instances, such as green milkweed (*Asclepias viridis*), a floral tinge of chartreuse

'Limelight' hydrangia

hardly seems humble against a background of ordinary leaf-green. Nor is there anything humble about the turquoise-green bracts of the Moroccan sea holly (*Eryngium varifolium*). Also, the creamy verdure of the 'Spring Green' tulip, the 'Emerald Spring' gladiola, the 'Lemon Lime' amaryllis, or the 'Limelight' hydrangea easily command second looks, as can the many variations of flowers with distinctly green stripes or throats.

Growing Green

Because green-flowered plants are considered exotic, they can be hard to find at garden centers. On the other hand, sometimes we simply fail to notice that they are already present in our gardens.

When grown as ornamentals, for instance, some vegetables offer decorative greenish flowers. Onions and leaks often produce attractive whitish-green flowerheads. Parsley is another example. Nor should we overlook our native prairie parsley (*Polytaenia nuttallii*), providing leaves and seeds that can be used like dill.

Bluebells (*Eustoma grandiflorum*), another Texas native plant, has unexpected apple-green and pale lime versions that insist on a second glance. A close look at passionflower (*Passiflora incarnata*), another

Lady's-slipper orchid (Paphiopedilum Maudiae 'Coloratum')

Texas native, reveals prominent green floral features at the center and edges. It is to be expected, then, that other passionflowers exhibit conspicuous green flowers, including the cute yellow passionflower (*P. lutea*), a bright-shade lover with flowers that can seem more green than yellow.

There are even green-accented rudbeckia coneflowers, such as verdant-bracted 'Green Wizard' and chartreuse-eyed 'Irish Eyes.' The uniqueness of *Echinacea* 'Green Jewel' refuses to be ignored. Flowering tobacco (*Nicotiana*), too, has lime-green selections, and verdant chrysanthemums include 'Feeling Green,' 'Shamrock,' and 'Green Satin.'

For repeat-blooming petunias that can endure Texas heat with afternoon shade, there are flamboyant pale green selections of hybrid petunias, including 'Surfinia Lime' and 'Sophistica Lime Bicolor.' Although coral bells (*Heuchera*) are usually prized for their showy leaves, 'Green Ivory,' 'Shamrock,' and 'Green Finch' feature whitish-green floral spikes.

Gardeners familiar with the South African torch lily or red poker plant (*Kniphofia*), an ideal option for Texas heat, might find the shimmery 'Green Jade' variety a bit impossible to believe at first glimpse. Less surprising for pond lovers are various green-flowered sedges, especially papyrus. And Texas xeriscapers have become increasingly enamored of the chartreuse blooms of the gopher plant (*Euphorbia rigida*).

The indoor plant-keeper should check out the Dallas Arboretum–approved 'Charmed Jade' oxalis, a short-termer with exquisite green-throated white flowers. For the longer term, there are various small cacti that strut bright green flowers. Green-accented, cream-hued flowers highlight *Pereskia aculeata*, a gorgeous West Indies rose descendant believed to be the ancestor of some cacti.

Orchid enthusiasts celebrate the stunning green-and-white lady's-slipper (*Paphiopedilum Maudiae* "Coloratum"). They have also cultivated gorgeous greenies among the fragrant cattleyas: for example, 'Elmhurst' with a red lip, 'Emerald Isle' with frilly petals, and 'Whirlpool' with a classic orchid elegance.

Kermit's complaint does not apply to plants. For them, including their flowers, it's easy being green. Yet the blooms we usually notice have ditched floral green for reasons we are still pondering.

≫ 15 ≪

Is My Contaminated Yard a Lost Cause?

While I was visiting at her home, a colleague showed me a bare garden plot adjacent to a side-yard fence. She wished she could grow a few vegetables in that spot. She had never done so because the close-by neighboring home had once been scraped in preparation for new paint. During that restoration, chips of the older paint had probably drifted into her yard, particularly the old veggie-patch segment. Ever since then, she worried about how much lead might have been deposited there.

Lead, it turned out, was not her only concern. She speculated that arsenic from the decaying pressure-treated lumber outlining the neglected plot had probably now saturated the surrounding soil. And she had still another worry: her home's previous owners had a long-standing contract with a pesticide company to routinely treat the property.

All of these potential hazards weighed on her mind. She could not help but consider how safe it would be to eat any vegetables grown in such ill-treated ground.

Lead

Lead is a potentially toxic metal that still makes its way into our yards despite government statutes reducing our exposure to it. It occurs naturally in some soils. It also gets into our yards and stays there, as my colleague suspected, from chips of pre-1978 leaded paint mingling with dirt. In a third and far more common way, lead accumulates on the ground from atmospheric emissions related to the years-ago combustion of leaded gasoline and some processes of industrialization.

The absence of lead from present-day paints and fuel does not mean that our home environments are now free from this metal. As an element, lead does not break down and can especially accrue near home foundations. It deposits there not only from older house paint but also (and more likely nowadays) from lead particles that are wind-blown from elsewhere (such as roadways). These particles strike and descend along house walls. Such deposited lead tends to remain close to the soil surface.

Since lead is not readily soluble, it is not easily absorbed by most plants. (Absorption refers to the movement of chemicals from outside to inside a plant.) Plant-uptake of lead is also generally inhibited in alkaline and organically enriched soils. Those plants capable of absorbing some lead, particularly in acidic soils with high amounts of the metal, deposit what they capture more in their leafy parts than in their fruiting parts.

Nevertheless, the possibility of lead clinging to plant surfaces from soil contact is much greater than finding lead deposited inside plant tissues. So, obviously, vegetables and fruits should be washed thoroughly, doubly so when grown close to foundations, roadways/driveways, or welded materials.

Arsenic

Arsenic is much more soluble and much more veggie-absorbable than lead. An issue of *Consumer Reports*, for example, alerted readers to the surprising levels of this carcinogenic metalloid in brown rice. Both inorganic and organic arsenic are (like lead) naturally occurring components of soil. Atmospherically dispersed arsenic, on the other hand, has been a by-product of fossil fuels, sundry chemical treatments, and some industrial processes.

Plant-uptake of arsenic is (as with lead) impeded by neutral-to-alkaline conditions and by organically enriched soil. Iron binds arsenic, too, forming a compound that is not usually available to plants. Also similar to lead, arsenic is more likely to show up in leaves and stalks rather than in fruits. Some veggies (such as tomatoes and lettuce) store this metalloid in their roots. Some root crops (including beets) store arsenic in the taproot skin, which can be peeled and discarded.

Green beans and other legumes are particularly sensitive to arsenic, which accumulates in their foliage and stunts their development. Washing thoroughly, obviously, is essential when dealing with both arsenic and lead contamination.

Pesticides

Until 2004 pesticides were the main source of arsenic found in pressure-treated lumber, and even today chromated copper arsenate (CCA) is still used in the production of some wooden items to ward off degradation by fungi and insects. Particularly in acidic settings CCA-treated wood leaches out these three chemicals during rainfall.

Plants absorb pesticides, which are then processed or stored or released into the ground and air. This can be true for even topical insecticides. Topical insecticides can be scrubbed away before eating a treated plant, but unfortunately "wash-off" by rain, hose flow, or transpiration can allow even topical chemicals to blend with the soil, where some of these chemicals might be absorbed into the plants. In this sense, topical insecticides can become somewhat systemic (distributed throughout a plant's tissues).

Systemic insecticides, of course, are designed to be tissue-pervasive in plants. Unfortunately, they fatally target good pollinators as well as pests. And if we eat these treated plants, we also ingest the pesticides.

Remedies

My colleague's situation has no quick remedy. She would have to start by inspecting for any indication of actual paint chips in the veggie plot's soil. Unless previously hoed/tilled under, these possible chips might still be close to the surface, which could be sanitized by a modest removal of surface soil.

Next a soil test of the remaining dirt would determine whether any toxic chemicals contaminate her inherited garden. If the report is disturbing, then her options include the laborious removal of even more tainted ground. Naturally, she would have to ensure that the replacement dirt is free from polluting chemicals.

Large containers or straw bales would allow her to avoid in-ground planting altogether. Another option—my favorite go-to choice when confronting inhibiting growing conditions—would be raised beds constructed after first removing any obvious surface contamination. If she built about a foot high, she could pretty much guarantee that shallow-rooted veggies, at least, will not access the dodgy dirt buried beneath the beds. Even so, before constructing the raised beds, she could work in plenty of organic matter and try to get the old plot soil a bit higher than pH neutral in order to immobilize lead and arsenic. Then, too, she would have to be sure that the new soil in the raised beds on top of the old section is free from any contaminants.

Phytoremediation

My colleague might also benefit from recent botanical research referred to as phytoremediation. Dr. Ilya Raskin, author of *Phytoremediation of Toxic Metals*, introduced this term to refer to plants that were unexpectedly cleaning up the Ukrainian Chernobyl reactor site after the terrible nuclear accident there on April 26, 1986. Today the word refers to various techniques (phytoextraction, phytovolatilization, phytodegradation, phytostabilization, rhizofiltration) utilizing plants to remove all manner of polluting chemicals from the air and the ground.

Consider our homes, where many volatile chemicals are said to have potential health-altering impacts on us. Formaldehyde can be especially problematic as it escapes from carpeting, laminate flooring, furniture, and similar products. Some houseplants, such as wax plant (*Hoya* sp.) and corn plant (*Dracaena fragrans*), have been reported to reduce ambient formaldehyde. Meanwhile, chrysanthemums and English ivies (*Hedera helix*) are said to reduce benzene, which volatilizes from synthetic fibers, plastics, and detergents. And Gerbera daisy and purple heart (*Setcreasea pallida*; previously *Tradescantia pallida*) appear to capture trichloroethane emanating from varnish, adhesives, and dry-cleaning chemicals. (I should mention that it is still scientifically unclear how well these and other plants perform as indoor cleaners, and some researchers have suggested that soil microbes nurtured by these plants are the actual purifiers of home pollutants.)

Outside our home we are usually more concerned about harmful metals. So far, bioremediation studies have identified and rated plants that aid in the removal of aluminum, silver, chromium, copper, manganese, mercury, selenium, and zinc, among other metals that have spoiled soils.

Phytoremediation works best when contamination levels are low.

Even then, it is a slow process often involving successive plantings over a number of years. It will not suit anyone in a hurry to get a poisoned space back into culinary production. But some bioremediation plantings in my colleague's "bad zone" would look better than barrenness. And while looking fine, these plants would actually be restoring her yard over the long term to allow for future plantings of culinary value.

One obstacle to a phytoremediation project in my colleague's Central Texas yard has been and would likely continue to be scarcity of rain. Most phytoremediation experiments have addressed sanitizing groundwater and wetlands, not droughty side-yards like hers. Phytoremediation works best with plenty of naturally available water, especially rain (which usefully tends to be acidic), to enable plant hydraulics to take up chemicals from the soil. The process is a kind of laundering, so to speak. Water is the medium for cleansing, while the plants function like filth-retaining washing machines that must eventually be discarded (not eaten or composted).

My colleague's yard had hardly been wet enough, often enough, to apply most researched phytoremedial plants. For instance, two species of duckweed (giant and minor) have been shown to take up lead. And the beautiful marsh-dwelling blue flag iris can clean up turf-type pesticides. Unfortunately, these plants will not work in a droughty landscape. Phytoremediation would be so much easier if my colleague's home were located in East Texas.

Nevertheless, she has excellent options. There are a few native, naturalized, and ornamental plants that are not habituated to moist settings but that nonetheless can undertake the cleanup of a Central Texas yard. Actually, all of these easy-to-grow plants can thrive in most of our state.

Grass versus Pesticides

A recent study reported in the *Journal of Environmental Quality* identifies two clumping grasses that serve as purifying vegetative filters for the fungicides, herbicides, and insecticides that are particularly associated with golf-course runoff. And it is especially good news for us that both of these plants—eastern gamagrass (*Tripsacum dactyloides*) and big bluestem (*Andropogon gerardii*)—are pervasive Texas natives.

Eastern gamagrass can produce four-foot-wide clumps and has adapted to a wide variety of soils in Texas. But it excels in fertile set-

Big bluestem

tings, creek edges, and other moist (not soggy) settings. So, as its common name suggests, it is a good candidate for pesticide remediation in East Texas.

Big bluestem, a rhizomed tallgrass-prairie perennial, would be a better option for my colleague's Central Texas yard. Big bluestem earns its name by reaching about five feet high and also stretching its roots many more feet down. It is sometimes used ornamentally as a year-round accent plant. Its attractive large clumps would easily thrive in most of our state. The cultivar 'Windwalker' is said to be better behaved—that is, less vigorously expansive—than typical of big bluestem.

Sunflowers versus Arsenic

While many plants absorb arsenic, not many so far have been rated as highly effective or efficient. A widespread Texas naturalized weed known as common bent grass or browntop (*Agrostis capillaris*) has shown promise. This disturbed-area invader thrives in moist settings, including meadows and roadsides, so it is not a prime candidate for droughty settings.

When it comes to cleaning up arsenic, Chinese ladder brake fern

Sunflowers

(*Pteris vittata*) is a hyperaccumulator capable of removing 25 percent of soil arsenic in about twenty weeks. Once its fronds become arsenic laden, even grasshoppers won't nibble them. This fern is acclimated to Texas, where it thrives in East Texas but has also naturalized statewide even in drier limestone conditions. Ferns are shallow-rooted, but that's all right because timber-leached arsenic contamination tends to remain concentrated near the soil surface. Ferns in my colleague's yard would need supportive watering and shading—from companioned big bluestem, perhaps—to prevent sunscald and desiccation.

While sunflowers and sorghum (the grain) are less impressive than this fern when extracting arsenic, both are easier to come by and to maintain in Texas. Since arsenic inhibits sunflower germination (with high concentrations being lethal), it is necessary to transplant established sunflowers to contaminated sites. Contaminant-uptake is augmented by slightly increasing soil acidity with ammonium sulfate or aluminum sulfate (as needed) and by adding some phosphorous (because arsenic moves through sunflowers' phosphate transporters).

Corn versus Lead

Sunflowers—the larger, the better—can take up lead as well as arsenic, a lesson learned from phytoremediation projects at Chernobyl and in post-Katrina New Orleans. Richly amending tainted ground with

Common corn

compost and manure not only nurtures sunflowers but also chemically enables them to "vacuum" effectively.

Common corn (*Zea mays*) has demonstrated an even more remarkable capacity for lead-uptake, which is stored primarily in its leaf and stalk tissues. This readily available crop is easy to grow and looks fine as a yard planting.

Besides common wheat, several widespread Texas weeds have demonstrated lead-extraction value, including Indian (brown) mustard (*Brassica juncea*), false indigo bush (*Amorpha fruticosa*), honey locust (*Gleditsia triacanthos*), and rattlebush (*Sesbania drummondii*). Ragweed (*Ambrosia* sp.) roots mine lead three times more effectively than corn roots, but I doubt that allergy sufferers will appreciate a nearby remediation project relying on this Texas native.

There is still another lead-cleanup option for droughty yards: ornamental (flowering) kale. Among its advantages, it thrives and looks beautiful throughout the winter, when other phytoremedial plants are not functional in most of Texas. It's an amazing gift when a plant meant to be a showy ornamental is also capable of invisible remedial heavy lifting.

≫ 16 ≪

Does The Moon Matter?

When planning a garden we primarily think about available sunlight. In fact, plants are routinely rated on labels and in guidebooks as requiring full sun, partial sun, bright shade, or full shade.

Our gardening calendar is also sun-based. We perceive four seasons cycling between two solstices when the sun is positioned farthest from the equator. In Texas we experience these solar extremes as the longest night on (roughly) December 21 and the longest day, the so-called first day of summer, on June 21.

Moon

But the sun is only one of the major celestial "players" in our sky. The other is the moon, and anyone who has been fascinated by ocean tides or animal behavior or werewolf legends knows that the moon is no smalltime player in earthly affairs.

So it isn't surprising that there is a long history of alternative calendars based primarily on the phases of the moon. The Chinese New Year, for example, begins with the second new moon appearing after the winter solstice, occurring in early February. And instead of a mere four seasons, old Chinese almanacs divide a year into seventy-two stages of five-day units related to the moon's cycles.

The full moon of our September is, for instance, understood as the fifteenth night of the lunar cycle, a date traditionally associated with harvesting. It's a time for celebration in Chinese, Korean, Vietnamese, and other cultures, and it is also the origin of the round, festive, fruit-and-nut mooncakes I can never resist at Chinatown bakeries in San Francisco.

Lunar gardening shouldn't be confused with creating a moon garden. A moon garden, which we will consider later, is designed for special visual and olfactory effects to be savored in twilight or at night. Lunar gardening, in contrast, refers to efforts to coordinate *every* activity in the garden with the phases of the moon. For some lunar gardeners, this activity is also aligned with the moon's perceived "journey" through the stellar constellations.

Plant Tides

The principal idea behind lunar gardening is easy to understand. Just as the moon influences sea tides, it presumably also affects the "tidal" motion of water in plants and soil. The ebb and flow of this water, lunar gardeners believe, have an impact on seed germination, floral development, and fruit production.

The lunar cycle, which runs 29.5 days, divides into two stages. In the waxing phase, the moon becomes increasingly visible until it is "full." In the waning phase, the moon progressively diminishes until it becomes "new." The position of the new moon between the earth and the sun almost obscures it from our sight. "See its slim shape," wrote the legendary Japanese poet Bashô, "It is as yet undeveloped, / the new moon, this night."

Lunar gardeners pay special attention to this sequence of the moon's phases. They believe that moisture in the ground becomes most available to plants during a full moon. At this lunar point, plants are thought to absorb more water than at other times. So, lunar gardeners maintain, seed will be most viable during the periods leading to a full moon.

Waxing and Waning

While this seems straightforward enough, lunar gardening is actually more complicated. The lunar waxing and waning stages are each subdivided into two seven-day, quarter-moon segments.

The seed of most annuals, lunar gardeners contend, should be planted during the moon's waxing phrase. The first seven days are thought to be particularly ideal for planting vegetables yielding aboveground fruit with exposed seeds, such as asparagus, mustard, bok choy, kale, cabbage, broccoli, and cauliflower.

The second week of the waxing cycle is said to be perfect for starting crops bearing aboveground fruit with enclosed seeds—tomatoes, okra, peppers, and melons, for example. During both waxing quarters, the incremental increase of moonlight stimulates the production of foliage.

A waning moon's diminishing light, on the other hand, retards flowering and benefits roots. So lunar gardeners plant bulbs, perennials, and underground vegetables—including radishes, carrots, and garlic—during the first seven days of a waning moon. They do so at this lunar stage because these plants need to become well established below the soil's surface.

The second week of the moon's decreasing light—the fourth quarter—is considered to be the best time for controlling insects, pruning, watering, and harvesting crops.

Constellations

Some lunar gardeners follow a still more complex scheme based on various astrological positions of the moon. Here matters get very complicated, and not only because of conflicting moon-gardening theories.

Every two to three days in the course of its monthly cycle the moon passes through one of the twelve constellations of the zodiac. Half of these stellar constellations—Aquarius, Aries, Gemini, Leo, Virgo, and Sagittarius—are described as barren. As a rule, planting should be postponed when the moon is in these unproductive constellations even if the lunar quarter is advantageous.

The remaining constellations are said to be fruitful (Pisces, Cancer, Libra, and Scorpio) or semifruitful (Taurus and Capricorn). Planting is advised when the moon passes into one of these productive constellations and is, at the same time, in a favorable phase for a specific species.

Precisely what activities are prescribed during this advantageous conjunction of stars and lunar phase depends on which theory is being followed. Complexity of calculation compounds when, as some moon-gardening calendars instruct, planetary positions are also factored into the regimen.

Fact or Fiction?

Is lunar gardening a matter of science or science fiction? Unfortunately, there isn't much reliable research to provide any clear answer.

But given what we know about the moon's influence on animal reproduction and on the earth's oceans, it seems reasonable to suspect that the moon can affect the "tidal motions" of both moisture in the ground and cellular fluids in plants. It is also very likely that the availability of moonlight stimulates the growth of aboveground crops. Research shows that even street lighting does that, so much so in fact that it can detrimentally stress plants by preventing normal rest periods.

As for claims about the vegetative impact of the position of the moon in relation to each of the twelve constellations—who knows what's fact or fantasy? Do we have to know for sure before enjoying a garden planted to benefit from the light of the moon? Perhaps there is something to be said for not trying to demystify all the secrets of the moon.

This much is certain: the moon inspires our imagination—a fact Mark Twain humorously acknowledged in *The Adventures of Huckleberry Finn*. While pondering the mysterious origin of stars, Huck considers the peculiar possibility that "the moon could a laid" the stars just as a chicken lays eggs. Huck decides, "Well, that looked kind of reasonable, so I didn't say nothing against it, because I've seen a frog lay most as many, so of course it could be done."

Huck is hilariously wrong. What he gets right, though, is a sense of wonder about the moon, which has always exerted a powerful influence on our imagination—still today, many decades after we first set foot on it. Lunar gardening is certainly imaginative, but this fact does not undermine its plausible emphasis on the impact of lunar phases on our plants.

Moon Gardening

Lunar gardening should not be confused with moon gardening, which refers simply to plants cultivated for our evening or nocturnal enjoyment. When (as a young man) I first heard the expression "moon garden," it sounded a little strange—and I was not at the time even thinking of peculiar notions about the moon's influence on gardens. Eventually I would dabble in so-called moonflowers and developed a self-satirical take on what had proved odd about them to me personally. In my case, moonflowers were exotic not because they seemed unusual but because they tended to bloom out of my sight while I was elsewhere, either indoors or asleep.

Moon gardens and I operated on different life-schedules. So I missed their flowering again and again as if they were far away in some foreign land instead of in my yard and glasshouse. It would have taken a certain determined resolve to alter my lifestyle a bit to catch these plants at their magnificent best. Over time, however, different huskies in my life imposed an early-morning regimen that fixed the problem for me. Their insistence on a neighborhood run (when I was younger) or walk (when I was older) well before sunrise everyday, regardless of weather, guaranteed that I would no longer miss out on my moonflowers' performances, at least in my front yard. I now think of these white flowers as night-garden morning stars.

Predawn mornings, it turns out, are good times to observe these plants, including freebie stalked rain lilies (*Zephyranthes* sp.). Of course, some people get to enjoy "moon plants" on patios during early evening, too. Frequently, however, these plants are at their prime at night, when their shape, size, scent, and color (commonly whitish or pale-hued) appeal to pollinators, particularly beetles, moths, and bats.

Four-O'Clocks

The multicolored, sweet-scented trumpets of four-o'clocks (*Mirabilis* sp.) top my list of favorite moonflowers. Whatever their color, they live up to the various translations of their Latin name *Mirabilis*, meaning wonderful, marvelous, extraordinary.

Once established, four-o'clocks take care of themselves. They are not fussy about soil, though their performance is enhanced by filtered shade during the day and by watering during dry spells to prevent wilting. These perennials bloom readily with minimal care and, if they die to the ground in winter, quickly revive in the spring.

Four-o'clocks, also known as marvel-of-Peru and beauty-of-the-night, roused Thomas Jefferson's curiosity. Later their appeal quickly spread throughout the United States during the nineteenth century. By the 1890s these night-bloomers were considered heirloom plants. An 1895 issue of *Garden and Forest* nostalgically promoted them as cherished old-fashioned plants reminiscent of grandmothers' gardens.

But the popularity of four-o'clocks declined during the twentieth century. It's hard to pinpoint precisely why. Perhaps smaller suburban home landscapes were not suitable for fast-spreading, three-foot bushes with leggy, easily broken branches. Or perhaps a weakening sense of tradition, a general preference for day-bloomers, and the allure of an ever-increasing array of new garden selections contributed to gardeners' loss of interest in four-o'clocks.

It is possible, as well, that as these plants naturalized in the wild—they can be invasive—they came to be seen merely as tough reseeding weeds. Their drought-tolerant, carroty taproots resist containment

Heirloom four o'clocks

and extraction. When pulled up, part of the root often remains in the ground and develops into a new plant. Personally, I am grateful that they are this tough, but other gardeners might easily not agree.

Today there is a modest revival of interest in four-o'clocks as heirlooms. Baker Creek Heirloom Seeds, for instance, has offered several selections of *M. jalapa* and *M. longiflora*. In an effort to preserve and promote open-pollinated antique flowers, Select Seeds has marketed these four-o'clock varieties: 'Alba,' 'Marrakesh' (rare), 'Limelight' (rare), and 'Salmon Sunset.' Seed Savers Exchange, a nonprofit organization saving and sharing genetically diverse heirlooms, has preserved an unnamed mixed-hued variety. 'Broken Colors' and 'Teatime,' both sometimes available from Renee's Garden, also produce bicolored and randomly patterned floral trumpets.

Angel's Trumpets

Angel's trumpets (*Brugmansia* sp.) are probably better known to Texas gardeners, but for most of us these south-of-the-border tender perennials are less hardy than four-o'clocks. I have seen them prevail as in-ground plantings in San Antonio and southward. Farther north, Jimmy Turner (while serving as senior director of gardens at the Dallas Arboretum) once told me that, with plenty of water and fertilizer, he had good success outdoors with apricot-trumpeted 'Charles Grimaldi,' a fragrant multicrossed brug hybrid.

Although there are only seven species of wild angel's trumpets, the number of commercial brug hybrids is overwhelmingly diverse. Guessing which cultivars will perform well outdoors in our state isn't easy. If you are unwilling to gamble with your brugs, use containers four feet wide and deep. Large draining planters with gravel at the bottom will stabilize angel's trumpets by countering their tendency to be top-heavy with foliage and blooms.

Widely cultivated *B.* × *candida* cultivars—often bearing unpoetic names such as 'Pink,' 'Ocre,' 'Rosea,' or 'Double White'—are rated as cold-hardy in most of Texas. White-hued 'Cypress Gardens,' another scented *B.* × *candida* selection, bears unusually long trumpets. Daintily ruffled 'Frosty Pink,' one of the *B. suaveolens* parents of 'Charles Grimaldi,' is also a beautiful possibility.

Devil's Trumpets

Until 1973, every *Brugmansia* was classified as a *Datura*. Although both are closely related members of the nightshade family (*Solanaceae*), you don't have to be a botanist to tell these fragrant night-bloomers apart. Datura trumpets stand upright or lean somewhat, while brugmansia flowers hang downward, and the intensity of their floral color as well as their scent can be compromised by outdoor temperature change. Both can also be distinguished by their stems. Brug branches are woody, while datura's are soft and green.

Eventually other differences appear. Angel's trumpets (*Brugmansia* sp.) are perennials and, in suitable environments, grow much taller than devil's trumpets (*Datura* sp.). Daturas are annuals or sometimes biennials limited to about five feet in height. Variation in fruit presents another clear distinction. Datura produces "thorn apples," a popular name for spherical, usually spined seed capsules. Angel's trumpets tend to produce elongated, fleshy fruits without spines.

As Texas wildflowers, various species of datura (including naturalized *D. metel* and *D. inoxia*) are well adapted for survival throughout our state. Their primary needs are well-drained, composted sandy or loamy locations, either somewhat acidic or alkaline, drenched in sunlight. Accustomed to dry conditions, they (unlike angel's trumpets) prefer little water.

Three particularly attractive varieties of *D. metel* are commonly available and easily grown outside. These include *fastuosa* with "double" purple flowers, *chlorantha* with "double" yellow trumpets, and *rubra* with "single" violet-fringed blooms. Annual seed for white-flowered *D. inoxia*, commonly referred to as jimsonweed, is often available at nonprofit plant sales or seed exchanges. More unusual datura cultivars, best grown in planters, include white 'Alba,' yellow 'Aurea,' violet 'Cornucopaea,' and dwarf bicolor 'Ballerina.'

Moonvines

Moonvines (*Ipomoea alba*) are large-flowered members of the morning-glory group. Unlike typical morning glories, though, moonvines bloom at dusk rather than dawn. "Victorian ladies filled their night-blooming gardens with these large, jasmine-scented flowers,"

Lynn Coulter has observed in *Gardening with Heirloom Seeds*. "The blooms unfurl like white parasols at dusk or on overcast days."

A trellis or other support is useful for these fifteen- to thirty-foot vines with attractive heart-shaped foliage and six-inch-wide flowers. Like night-fragrant vining petunias (*P. multiflora*), however, moonvines can be left to scramble. Moonvines are technically perennials, but generally these south-of-the-border natives are treated as annuals in our state.

Like other types of morning glory, moonvines can be grown from seed available at garden centers. And, incidentally, the word across the backyard fence is that their seed should be soaked for two days before being planted.

Flowering Tobacco

South American or flowering tobacco (*Nicotiana* sp.) is widely available at Texas plant outlets, but the original night-blooming versions might be harder to find as potted plants. Plant breeders have invested heavily in shorter, more compact, day-flowering nicotinanas, usually at the cost of the original plant's fragrance.

For night-bloomers, look for (Brazilian) winged-tobacco (*N. alata*), (Argentine) woodland tobacco (*N. sylvestris*), and (Chilean) star petunia (*N. longiflora*). 'Aztec Sweet,' a dusk-fragrant and old-time variety of flowering tobacco, is an heirloom.

Long bouts of dryness are not easy on flowering tobacco, which needs water to stay healthy, stand upright, and flower. Often these highly fragrant night-bloomers keep their floral trumpets open during the morning, too, although by that time their scent tends to be lost. They should be treated as shade plants benefitting from bright indirect light. Although technically a perennial, in Texas flowering tobacco is usually treated as an annual.

Cacti, Zinnias, and More

There are night-blooming cacti that thrive outdoors in most of Texas, both in pots and in the ground. They are so easy to grow and require such minimal maintenance that there is little more to be said about them other than their names. Among the favorites in our yard are orchid cacti (*Epiphyllum* sp.), often mistaken as night-blooming

Night-blooming orchid cactus (Epiphyllum strictum)

cereus. It grows many sprawling, broad, flattened, and easily propagated branches reaching several feet in length. Another of our favorites is
an actual night-blooming cereus (probably *Cereus peruvianus*), which
features a more conventional fleshy columnar cactus form.

There are also flowering plants that are not night-bloomers but
that "shine" in moonlight. We particularly like cream-hued marigolds
and also dahlia-like zinnias, such as 'Classic White' and old-fashioned
'Polar Bear.' And consider, too, plants with bright silvery foliage.
Dusty miller (*Senecio cineraria*), lamb's ear (*Stachys byzantina*), Japanese painted fern (*Athyrium niponicum* var. *pictum*), Russian sage,
(*Perovskia atriplicifolia*) ghost plant (*Artemisia schmidtiana* 'Silver
Mound') and sea holly (*Eryngium* sp.), among others, all "glow" in
moonlight.

When thinking about a moon garden or any other ornamental
planting, keep in mind (as mentioned previously) that many popular plants—ficus, oleander, lily of the valley, and hydrangea, among
countless others—produce various chemicals designed to deter other
plants as well as to ward off foraging animals. Such toxic chemical
production is particularly true of the nightshade family, which includes
the moon-garden favorites *Datura*, *Brugmansia*, and *Nicotiana*. All
parts of these nightshades contain tropane alkaloids, which are poi-

Datura metel fruit

sonous if eaten. Texas AgriLife Extension has reported that animals consuming relatively small amounts of such plants—a mere 1 percent of an animal's body weight—have died. So safeguard children and pets from these otherwise lovely night-blooming plants.

And speaking of children, perhaps you recall my daughter, who once literally asked me for the moon. Only she can answer whether, some years later in her life, she settled for a couple of late-evening visits to a patch of moonlit night-bloomers. Each time I had to promise, more than once, that there would be no vampires lurking in the shadows. Luckily on those occasions no unseen owl flew close by, its feathers winging a sudden muffled whoosh that is always a bit startling in the gloaming before pitch-dark.

Chapter 16

Gardeners Who Shared

17

Devil Cactus Makes Good

Mention "cactus" to Texans, and more likely than not they will imagine a prickly pear. To most of us a prickly pear is—well, heck—a prickly pear. What else is there to know about this ubiquitous spiny menace with pretty flowers? We mistakenly tend to use the expression "prickly pear" in a general sense, referring to what actually is a variety of different padded species of *Opuntia*, the genus name for these cacti.

It's been that way for a long time. Riding "through a Texas pear flat," a famous short-story author wrote, is "more weird and lonesome than

Opuntia macrorhiza with uncommon lemon-cream hued flowers

the journey of an Amazonian explorer": "With dismal monotony . . . the uncanny and multiform shapes of the cacti lift their twisted trunks, and fat, bristly hands to encumber the way. The demon plant . . . warps itself a thousand times about what look to be open and inviting paths, only to lure the rider into blind and impassable spine-defended 'bottoms of the bag.'"

This description of wild prickly pears appears in "The Caballero's Way," a story by O. Henry. Having lived in Texas for a while, O. Henry knew firsthand about the menace of these native succulents. Prickly pears are no less problematic on today's ranches, which is why Dave Gross in Oglesby, Texas, invented the Kactus Krusher. Dragged behind a tractor, this hefty machine mows, shreds, and crushes prickly pears while minimally damaging native grasses.

Is there any hope for this spiny nuisance that pioneer Texans disparaged as "devil cactus"? Yes, apparently. Prickly pear has traditionally served as a property security barrier in Mexico, and its fleshy pads have been known to retard the spread of fire in areas made vulnerable by drought. Prickly pear has also long been a favorite subject for Lone Star painters. Today, too, it has increasingly become a garden option valued for its look, endurance, and low maintenance. This is quite a change in status for O. Henry's formidable "demon plant."

Prickly Specifics

Opuntia appears in two shapes: cylindrical and padded. The cylindrical types are known as chollas, the padded as prickly pears. Both produce attractive fruits—usually yellow for chollas and purple-red for prickly pears. Despite their fruits, both types tend to reproduce by root expansion or fallen pads.

Prickly pear is native only to the Americas, but the number of its species remains unknown. In fact, the South American members of *Opuntia* have barely been identified, much less studied. To complicate matters, *Opuntia* species readily crossbreed. So new hybrids appear frequently in the wild. While such easy hybridization impedes efforts at scientific classification, it also provides opportunities for plant growers to reproduce naturally occurring novel varieties for ornamental use.

Sometimes a prickly pear species will produce multiple versions (mutations). This is the case with *O. robusta*, a treelike and multibranched Mexican cactus capable of reaching nearly ten feet high.

This fiendishly spined plant occasionally produces spineless variations, and these deviations from the norm have become the sources for handsome garden selections of this plant.

Prickly Blooms and Pads

The color of prickly pear flowers also varies. The low-growing beavertail cactus (*O. basilaris*), which can be spineless, flaunts striking flowers ranging from bright yellow to cherry red. The plains prickly pear (*O. macrorhiza*), which ranges southward from the Midwest, commonly produces yellow flowers. But in this case the word "yellow" is inadequate to convey the various possible floral shades of this hue. The flowers can be reddish-yellow, orange-yellow, lemon-yellow, or cream-yellow.

Also making a dramatic statement in the garden, prickly pear pads vary in tint, shape, and size. The pads of the black-spined prickly pear (*O. macrocentra*), for example, turn mauve-green when stressed by cold or drought. The Santa Rita candle cactus (*O. santa-rita*), native to the Southwest, forms violet-purple pads as well as yellow flowers

Black-spined Opuntia macrocentra

with red throats. The Texas native succulent popularly known as old man whiskers (*O. aciculata*), also marketed as chenille prickly pear, offers eye-catching patterns defined by wide-spaced spines on its pads. It produces gorgeous orangey-red glochids, which are small hairy clusters of modified spines.

For zany garden accents there are several varieties of cow's tongue cactus (*O. engelmannii*), famous for the unusual shape of its pads and infamous for its capacity to colonize plowed or overgrazed areas. One variety of this Texas native, *linguiformis*, develops elongated pads of various lengths adorned with single long spines and attractive auburn glochids. Another former variety, now considered a separate species (*O. lindheimeri*), sprawls untidily and forms typical pads shaped like paddles as well as extremely odd-shaped pads looking like cows' tongues. The yellow spines of this cactus lack the auburn spiny clusters of *linguiformis*.

Prickly Uses

Prickly pears, which require virtually no maintenance, bring more to the garden than flowers, pads, and spines. They also bring history.

Prickly pears were used by Native Americans to treat various ailments, including coughs and rheumatism. The Pima Indians used cow's tongue cactus to aid nursing women; the Navajo used the black-spined prickly pear for medical lances; and the Shoshoni used the beavertail cactus as a poultice for wounds.

Over the centuries, the pads and fruits of these cacti provided food for humans and animals alike—and not just during bad times. Today, too, prickly pear pads (nopalitos) are still used in delicious salads, soups, casseroles, chilis, salsas, preserves, and even desserts.

O. ficus-indica, the so-called Indian fig from Mexico, is the most common source for culinary pads. Harvested pads should be young, small, tender, and bright green. Of course, glochids must be cut out of the harvested pad before preparing it for eating. By the way, if an inch or so of stub is left on the plant from which the pad has been harvested, a new pad will likely form.

Fruits, which vary wildly in quality and are often quite sour, should be harvested with tongs when they are maximally ripe—usually (for *O. lindheimeri*) when they turn a deep purple-red. Ripe fruits of *O. ficus-indica* and related prickly pears range in color from white to yellow to orange. When carefully peeled, cacti fruits can be eaten raw or cooked.

Also with tradition in mind, the "Old Mexico" cultivar should not to be overlooked. This fast-growing, four-foot South Texas pass-along, suitable for hardiness zones 8 to 10, produces large spineless pads that have traditionally been used to make long-lasting Christmas wreaths. Its many radiant yellow flowers are also a sight to behold.

Wicked Beauty for North-Central Texas

"Wicked Beauty!" That's Irwin Lightstone's personal name for *Opuntia microdasys*, a particularly striking prickly pear capable of surviving outdoors in North Central Texas.

A retired trial attorney who lives in Dallas, Irwin has learned all about "Wicked Beauty" and its near and distant relatives during his many years of membership in the North Texas Cactus and Succulent Society. This organization, founded in 1974 and holding sessions open to curious nonmembers, promotes the study and enjoyment of succulents in both native habitats and home landscapes.

Irwin has found prickly pears to be alluring, even addictive. It's easy to fall for *Opuntia microdasys*, he told me. This Mexican prickly pear produces deep green pads ornamented by gorgeous clusters of tiny needle-sharp glochids.

So it's not surprising that it has acquired several pretty-sounding common names, including golden wave, angel's wings, bunny ears, and polka-dot cactus. The name golden wave refers to varieties of this species with especially curvy pads bearing yellow glochids. Other varieties with more conventionally shaped pads produce yellow, white (var. *albaspina*), or rust-red (var. *rufidula*) glochids.

Whatever the variety or cute name, every *Opuntia microdasys* is "Wicked Beauty" as far as Irwin is concerned. What's easy on the eyes, he insisted, can be brutal to the hands.

"I've tried everything I could think of—tweezers, duct tape, and even coating my fingers with a film of Elmer's glue—but the burning tiny spines always break off under my skin." By photographing the plant closeup, he found that these miniscule spines are designed to break away easily from the plant with the slightest touch.

Even so, "Wicked Beauty" is a keeper, Irwin maintained. And so are various hedgehog cacti. "They have fantastic flowers and spines." For in-ground plantings as far north as Dallas and Fort Worth, Irwin

Claret-cup cactus (Echinocereus triglochidiatus)

recommended three Texas-native hedgehog cacti: *Echinocereus dasya-canthus* with yellow-to-orange flowers, *E. reichenbachii* with pink-to-purple flowers, and *E. triglochidiatus* with orange-to red flowers.

Thelocactus bicolor also ranks high on his list of in-ground favorites. Commonly known as glory of Texas, this spectacular cactus offers attractive red and white spines as well as bright magenta flowers.

Ferocactus, which includes about twenty-nine barrel species native to North American deserts, are particularly enduring as landscape plants. Their bee-pollinated flowers are showy, and they also offer fascinating variations in spine patterning. Just don't bump into their "fishhooks."

Such native cacti are capable of surviving temperature lows to 10 degrees—the cold-hardiness range for the Dallas–Forth Worth area as indicated on the latest version of the USDA plant zone map. But this does not make them foolproof, Irwin cautioned.

Hardiness is not just a matter of being able to withstand temperature lows, he pointed out. "Hardiness depends on several factors interacting with temperature, such as exposure, moisture, and drainage. Unlike many foliage plants, often cacti can survive colder temperatures better when their soil is dry rather than when wet."

How to Succeed by Trying

Irwin offered these other tips for success. "The key to healthy outdoor cacti is to raise their beds and ensure exceptional drainage. More cacti are lost due to poor drainage than to cold weather." It is also beneficial to position cacti on a slight slope.

Irwin has found that cacti facing south tend to stay warmer and so do better than those facing north. Overhead protection can help, such as "shelter beneath larger plants or a fence or wall for protection from north winds." This is particularly true for various cacti not native to North Central Texas. "Many of the non-*Opuntia* cacti grow in grassland or receive at least some shade during the day."

When pressed for a final bit of advice about zone-pushing prickly pears, Irwin paused, then offered a knowing take on all gardening endeavors: "Hope for a little luck."

18

Salvia Fever

No medical text lists salvia fever as an ailment.

But don't tell that to John Rembetski. He has personally seen what salvia fever can do. He has seen it transform both the front and rear yards of his Central Austin home—including patio, stairs, and driveway—into a dense collage of hardy salvias, or sages, as they are commonly called. Now only John knows the way through this maze of plants. And occasionally even he struggles to detect a path during my visit.

"It isn't landscaped in the conventional sense," John apologized as he carefully lifted foliage to find where we should step during one of my visits.

How It Started

It wasn't always like this for him. John can remember a time before salvia fever, a time when he bought a house with a typical ho-hum landscape. That changed in 1994, when an assortment of sages at Chip Schumacher's plant nursery in New Braunfels were simply too tempting for him to resist.

John purchased many different varieties that, he said, he "instantly popped" into his yard. At the same time he received seed for other sage selections from Seedhunt in California. Then a friend in San Antonio caught salvia fever during a West Coast visit and returned with a number of hard-to-propagate sages that she shared with John.

Salvia fever is contagious, spreading easily through such garden exchanges. John admitted, however, that earlier in his life he already showed signs of this affliction. Even as a child he liked to collect and

Salvia farinacea 'Rhea'

grow plants from seeds and cuttings given to him by a grandmother and an uncle.

That was child's play compared with his adult garden pursuits. These days John conducts homegrown salvia experiments that, he believes, parallel the protocols used during his career as a plasma-etching engineer in the semiconductor industry. John, who has reported his findings to local nurseries, has been surprised by how many zone 10 sages (which normally live in the USDA cold-hardiness range for Brownsville) manage to survive Austin's worst winters. He shares the successful plants with other salvia enthusiasts.

What He Learned

Salvias, John explained, require soils with excellent drainage. Silver-leafed sages require full-sun exposure. Small-leafed sages, such as ever-popular *S. greggii*, need more sun than shade; whereas large-leafed sages, such as *S. puberula*, perform best with afternoon shade and extra water. Dry-land or desert salvias should be mulched with gravel rather than root-rotting organic matter.

Through trial and error, John has identified *Salvia microphylla* 'Hot Lips' as an especially excellent cultivar for sunny locations. This sage displays red-and-white blooms primarily during spring and autumn. For part-sun, John favored hard-to-find *S. caudata* 'El Cielo Blue,' bearing shiny leaves and exquisite flowers. He also highly recommended equally beautiful 'Blue Chiquita,' an autumn-winter bloomer with twenty-inch floral spires.

He has had good experiences as well with two other Mexican natives: blue-flowered germander sage (*S. chamaedryoides*) and red-flowered southern Mexican sage (*S. disjuncta*). *Salvia puberula*, a rare south-of-the-border sage, also graces John's garden with prominent magenta-hued blooms.

Garden Bats and Firecrackers

Among his salvias John has sprinkled a variety of other plants, such as the Texas native blue waxweed (*Cuphea viscosissima*). John believes that cupheas (pronounced kew-FAY-ahs) enhance his salvia gardens.

Since most wild cupheas range from Mexico to Brazil, they withstand our challenging summer heat. In fact, Southwest plant expert Mary Irish reports that they manage to endure summers in Phoenix, Arizona. Many established cupheas also easily survive our winters in East, South Central, and South Texas, where they often grow back if they happen to be lightly frozen to the ground. Texas AgriLife Extension recommends various cupheas as xeriscape possibilities particularly ideal for the coastal regions of our state and also the El Paso area.

However, most cupheas have small taproots. So during prolonged periods of dryness they tend to be susceptible to stress—manifested by wilting and leaf drop. On the other hand, although their upkeep in our state may require periodic hydration—as do salvias, for that matter—their small root systems are satisfied with only a moderate amount of water. They also need good drainage and benefit from composting and mulching.

Mexican or false heather (*C. hyssopifolia*), also known as elfin herb, forms dainty small bushes bearing short-stemmed clusters of miniature flowers. Petal color is typically dark pink, but shades vary between pink-purple ('Allyson') and white ('Alba'). 'Alba,' incidentally, supports its flowers on thin, strikingly red stems.

In John's Central Texas locale Mexican heather sometimes serves as a year-round in-ground plant. Although its floral show fluctuates with the weather, it tends to perform well from late spring until the first or second wintery freeze. Then it commonly dies to the ground unless it enjoys an advantageous microclimate. One winter, which was colder than usual in the Austin area, saw the demise of many in-ground Mexican heathers, especially those less than a year old. Plants close to structural foundations generally did better throughout that wintry ordeal.

Established Mexican heather that has died to the ground typically revives in spring and then easily tolerates our summer heat. It performs best when directly exposed to only morning sunlight. Like most cupheas, it endures dry stretches but becomes stressed by prolonged dehydration. So watering this cutie, as needed, will keep it showy.

The firecracker or cigar plant (*C. ignea*)—not to be confused with firecracker fern (*Russelia equisetiformis*)—has also become an in-ground success story in the southern half of Texas. Its hummingbird-attracting floral features are distinguished by reddish calyxes (whorled modified leaves at a flower base). The "cigar flowers" are commonly orange-red with an ashy-white rim and two tiny purple accents. Fuchsia-bright 'Pink Flamingo,' buff-hued 'Petite Peach,' cream-yellow 'Lutea,' and yellow-pink 'Triple Crown,' among other selections, offer variations on the *C. ignea* theme.

I've seen this small cuphea begin blooming in late spring, but usually it comes into its own during summer. Although firecracker plant is a little less compact and tidy than Mexican heather, it is easy to manage. Like Mexican heather, it suffers leaf damage during freezes and sometimes dies completely to the ground. It sprouts again in the spring, particularly if it was lightly mulched over winter. Also like Mexican heather, firecracker plant performs optimally with periodic watering and with protection from direct exposure to afternoon summer sunlight.

Beautiful 'David Verity,' likely a cross between *C. ignea* and *C. micropetala*, has scored at the top of various plant trials. It is taller than firecracker plant, and its orange calyxes are rimmed by yellow and green petals. Bee-loving 'Starfire' is an extremely attractive and resilient hybrid resulting from crossing *C. ignea* and *C. angustifolia*, a Mexican wildflower. The eye-catching fuchsia calyxes of 'Starfire' parade lavender and white petals—a rich enhancement of the firecracker plant's plainer ashen rim.

Bat-faced or tiny-mice cuphea (*C. llavea*) sprawls more than firecracker plant or Mexican heather, but that hasn't kept it from becoming highly popular. The reason is no mystery: a sensational multicolored floral display looking like "the mouth of a bat, with red Mickey Mouse ears"—Mary Irish's playfully apt description of the plant in *Perennials of the Southwest*.

It's a prolific bloomer, too, with the same requirements as most cupheas: drainage, compost, mulch, and adequate moisture. In the region shared by John and me, this two-footer has thrived and bloomed most of the year as an in-ground plant, especially when fully estab-

Bat-faced cuphea (C. llavea)

lished and also located on the northeastern side of a home for shelter from too much direct summer sunlight. It has worked well as an in-ground plant in the Austin area except for one year's unusually cold winter. While many in-ground bat-faced cupheas sustained only partial leaf damage until the onset of 20-degree nights, some succumbed at lower temperatures.

Colorful hybrids derived from this cuphea are legion. The most well known is *C.* × *purpurea*, which is a prized cross between bat-faced cuphea and creeping waxweed (*C. Procumbens*). 'Vienco Lavender' bears gorgeous two-toned purple flowers, while 'Firefly' and 'Georgia Scarlet' (also known as 'Tiny Mice') are cherry-red. 'Totally Tempted' has succeeded in my neighborhood, as has the flamboyant Flamenco series, which includes 'Cha Cha,' 'Rumba,' 'Samba,' and 'Tango.' The Dallas Arboretum ranked 'Rumba' as a top-ten annual.

Cuphea micropetala

'Plum Mist' is an unusual Mexican creeping cuphea (*C. rosea*) with dark-veined lavender petals. Capable of withstanding zero degrees F, this ten-inch-high plant is as pretty as it is tough. Purple blooms also distinguish 'Lavender Lace'—"a prostrate form, terrific in containers and falling out of raised beds," Allan Armitage has reported in *Armitage's Manual of Annuals, Biennials, and Half-Hardy Perennials.*

The candy-corn plant, on the other hand, is a tall, bushy cuphea (*C. micropetala*) potentially attaining a height of three feet or so. It is sometimes referred to as "old-fashioned cigar plant." *C. micropetala* tends to bloom better as the growing season advances, and its gangly stems benefit from a structural support.

C. cyanea is another tallish, somewhat lanky Mexican cuphea. Some gardeners report that as an in-ground plant this cuphea can be challenging to keep. Even so, a mere glance at the scarlet-"eared," yellow-striped, and tangerine blooms of 'Caribbean Sunset' suggests that the floral payoff for success with this cuphea is nothing less than an eye-pleasing spectacle.

No Cure

As much as John appreciates cupheas to fill in vacant garden spaces, for him sages are always the main attraction. When asked why he is so attached to salvias, John struggled for answers. It is, of course, an unreasonable question to ask any devotee. So our conversation easily drifted to related matters, such as the many sage "starts" growing inside his house, including his bathtub.

He also mentioned trips to Cabrillo College near Santa Cruz, California, where once or twice a year he has visited the largest collection of sages in the United States. There he has met with other salvia experts, including Betsy Clebsch, author of *The New Book of Salvias*: *Sages for Every Garden*.

"It took us so long to discuss each plant," John said of one August meeting of salvia aficionados at the college, "that we had to break for lunch and reconvene to continue the tour." After pausing for a moment, he added: "Much of the lunch discussion was more salvia talk."

At the end of our meeting I mentioned having seen several *Salvia azurea* plants growing wild in a prairie restoration project on the Shield Ranch near Westcave Preserve in southwest Travis County. John's eyebrows rose expectantly before he asked for directions. There is, it seems, no hope for his condition.

"Maybe a local strain," he speculated. "I should collect and propagate some of its seeds."

19

Ditching Callas for Daylilies and Irises

Because they commonly grace weddings, funerals, and religious services, calla lilies might seem to be thoroughly familiar plants. They do, in fact, have a long horticultural history in Europe, and they were introduced in North America during the nineteenth century and soon became fashionable enough to have draped President Lincoln's casket. Their popularity surged during the early twentieth century, when Georgia O'Keeffe also devoted entire canvases to lavish, sexually nuanced images of callas.

But if callas are very familiar today, there is much more to their bold and beautiful display than we generally know. Such as: they are not, in fact, actually lilies, nor are they any longer even considered to be callas—one more revision due to genetic studies. They are tender rhizomes and tubers from Africa that now belong to a small group of perennials classified as *Zantedeschia* (pronounced zan-tah-DES-key-ah), a close relative of caladiums and Jack-in-the pulpits (*Arisaema triphyllum*).

The number of *Zantedeschia* species remains uncertain. Whatever their number, they don't share common ground. The impressively tall, white-flowered calla lily (*Z. aethiopica*) so easily grown in moist garden settings and frequently used on festive occasions is, unfortunately, no guide to caring for the very fussy miniature cuties that can bewitch us with their exotic charm.

Irresistible Cuties

If you're like me, you have fallen for the enticing mini callas more than once while shopping at a garden center during early spring. Under a foot high, they dazzle with their sleek emerald leaves and radiant flowers.

A calla flower is actually a spathe, a modified leaf (bract) slightly curled around a central spike (spadix) of tiny blooms. Yellow-to-orange spathes usually distinguish the *Z. elliottiana* hybrids, which also tend to feature broad, heart-shaped foliage speckled with translucent whitish spots. Purple or pink spathes mostly occur among the *Z. rehmannii* hybrids, which also tend to produce lance-shaped, typically spotless foliage.

'Pink' mini callas

Bred for elegant compactness, graceful foliage, and spectacular floral contour and color, these exquisite hybrids are irresistibly alluring. And they are dirt-cheap—an impulse purchase just waiting to happen. It's all too easy to find yourself bringing home one or more of the little beauties.

Mad with Beauty

Once these novelty callas are in your home, ideally beside a sunny (untinted) window, perhaps a bit belatedly you wonder, "How do I take care of them?"

The tag, if there is one, is not going to help much. It states that the plant is a calla. Possibly it gives an enchanting hybrid name, such as 'Blaze,' 'Flame,' 'Fire Glow,' 'Sunshine,' 'Golden Chalice,' 'Parfait,' 'Crystal Blush,' 'Rose Gem,' or 'Pillow Talk'—an ever-growing imaginative list, it seems, of appealing poetic images designed to override anyone's rational hesitation.

The tag might also offer a few broad instructions about sunlight and water, but basically you are on your own with your lovely temperamental acquisitions. What likely ensues could make you sympathize with the plea of the heroine of William Morris's "The Defence of Guenevere": "I was half mad with beauty on that day."

Yeah. And the remaining half of that madness might not be far behind as you begin in earnest to cope with your diva minis.

Diva Devotion

The first mistake often made with mini callas is treating them as if they had the same needs as the old-fashioned white calla lily. The festive white calla bearing large floral chalices is the toughest of its kind and the easiest to maintain, provided its rhizomes are kept moist, cool, and unfrozen. Especially large cultivars are available, too, including 'White Giant' and 'Hercules.'

The flat, roundish tubers of the mini callas, in contrast, insist on considerably more drainage, and they tolerate added moisture only when their organically enriched soil is nearly dry. If they stay too wet, they rot and die; if they get too dry, these finicky divas will go prematurely dormant, like Sleeping Beauty.

Keeping mini hybrids' moisture level optimal is the biggest challenge, I have found. It is not an undertaking for the casual, preoccu-pied, or impatient caretaker, which (*confiteor*) too often I am.

Texas heat is another trying factor. Dormancy can be triggered by too much heat or by temperatures below 55 degrees. The minis need plenty of sunlight, but without the risk of desiccation or heat prostra-tion. This requirement makes these tropicals better houseplants than outdoor possibilities in our state.

An untinted eastern window with direct morning light should suit them during summer, whereas a southern window is better during winter. Note, though, that air blown through heating and air-conditioning vents can trigger mini-calla dormancy.

Regardless of close attention to these callas, the onset of dorman-cy can be unpredictable. In a calla hybrid's normal cycle, dormancy would occur during late summer. Then its (deciduous) foliage droops, yellows, and falls off the plant. With all their leaves gone over many months, mini callas will appear to be dead. But they aren't.

During their dormancy, maintaining soil conditions—not too dry, not too wet; not too hot, not too cold—is crucial to ensure the gen-eration of new foliage in early spring. At the first sign of revival, keep mini callas moist (not soggy) and exposed to direct morning sunlight.

At least the appetite of the divas by your window is not very big. Apply a low-nitrogen fertilizer, such as 5-10-5 or 5-10-10, when foliage first appears and then about four weeks later. Do not feed during any stage of blooming.

Flower-Girl Troubles

While I haven't found it difficult to get my mini callas to leaf out during spring, I have struggled to get them to reflower beyond their purchase year. Calla experts agree that these flower girls tend to be extraordinarily temperamental.

When not forced-bloomed for the March market, diva callas typi-cally flaunt their beauty sometime in May or June—that is, about eight weeks after new foliage has emerged. Nevertheless, their flowering can be unpredictable, determined by species genetics and by horticultural conditions.

A mistake I once made was moving my leafing callas to a deck in March so that they might benefit from direct morning sunlight. I had no trouble keeping them moist with reserved rainwater (not chemically treated tap water), but spring in Texas can too quickly become unseasonably hot. The swift onset of high temperatures that spring inhibited blooming and, worse, eventually induced dormancy. Since mini callas bloom in cooler temperatures, I should have kept mine indoors.

As fussy as mini callas are about temperature, moisture, and drainage, it is easy to suspect they would be equally finicky about root-crowding. Surprisingly, though, they perform best when moderately root-bound—a small break for their beleaguered caretakers, who at least don't have to fret about repotting them for some time.

Femmes Fatales

Keep in mind that the beauty of callas belies a potential danger. Like many other tropical plants, mini callas are poisonous if any part of them is ingested. They should be kept out of the reach of curious pets and children.

As we have seen, too, the low purchase price of mini callas belies their high demands. For impatient gardeners, they can be maddening femmes fatales. For gardeners in the know, on the other hand, these beauties can be a fascinating test of skill—a contest between human cunning and exotic tuber.

The easiest way to outwit mini callas is to simply enjoy them as annuals. They are so inexpensive that if they last for only a single season, their beauty has already repaid your small investment. Of course there is always the option of resisting the exotic beauty of mini callas in the first place and, instead, seeking out the equally exquisite but more accommodating charms of Texas-bred daylilies and irises.

Homegrown Daylilies

Daylilies (*Hemerocallis*) are hardly as fleeting as their everyday name suggests. Yes, each of their blooms lasts for only a single day. But the days turn into weeks while new flowers open one after another. And daylilies are long-lived, producing this spectacular floral sequencing over many years, even in untended areas such as roadsides.

Long-lasting daylilies can "plant" long-lasting memories, too. When I was a small child in the 1940s, for instance, roadside daylilies (*H. fulva*) fascinated me. They also led to a bit of humorous craziness between my father and me. While I thought wild daylilies were beautiful, he insisted they were just weeds. As an eight-year old, I transplanted a dozen around a maple tree in our side yard. Whenever my father hand-mowed the lawn, he deliberately cut down these "weeds." Eventually, these tough naturalized garden escapes increased and multiplied, and today they thrive where I planted them.

Daylilies figure also in one of Mark Carpenter's memories. "I'll never forget going up that dirt drive off Highway 7 and seeing over 50,000 flowers in bloom," Mark remembers about his first encounter with his uncle's daylily farm in Center, Texas, near Nacogdoches. "Beauty was around me everywhere, and people were shopping all around the three acres, and happiness was abundantly flowing all around me. Wow, I thought, this is a happy business!" Looking back on that moment now, he has realized that "the daylily bug" had hit him and hit him hard.

How hard? Well, whenever his uncle mentioned that someone was interested in purchasing the farm, Mark felt his "heart breaking ever so slightly" each time he heard about it. He wanted to take over the farm from his retiring uncle, but that would mean uprooting his family from San Antonio. What followed were "many, many hours of careful debate, prayer, deliberations, prayer, consultations, prayer, and then more prayer. Do I take my life's earnings and move my family to Nacogdoches to follow my dream?"

Perhaps in some mysterious way Mark's decision was already fated from his very first encounter with the place. Now he owns that twenty-five-year-old lily farm, one of the largest of such businesses in the United States.

Location, Location, Location

Mark had considered moving the farm to San Antonio. After all, he had hybridized daylilies, learned about their habits, and grew his own seedlings in his San Antonio backyard. All of that, however, was "on a very small, conservative scale," whereas "to run a commercial daylily business would be almost impossible." Too much heat and too little water were significant factors in his decision. "San Antonio sits over the Edwards Aquifer, and many say this is the largest fresh water aquifer in the United States. But San Antonio treats water the way Houston would treat oil. You pay for it, and you pay a lot. What about drilling a well? Good luck with that one, as the caliche ground in this area requires dynamite to get below it, and sometimes you are going down hundreds of feet to reach water."

As Mark's account suggests, daylilies perform best in Texas when their April-through-June blooming season is not hindered by drought or the premature onset of very high temperatures. Where you situate them in your yard matters, too. In fact, at the top of Mark's advice for daylily success is "location, location, location! Forget what you read on the Internet about daylilies loving full sun. Not in Texas! Cacti die here! Daylilies need full morning sun and really need full or at least partial afternoon shade. This is the single most important factor to successfully growing daylilies here."

'Chorus Line' daylilies

"Clay is impossible to grow daylilies in," Mark also pointed out. Instead, "build a raised bed. We use aged pine-bark mulch mixed into our natural sandy loam beds for our plants, and they love it. If you build a bed, the deeper the better because a deep bed allows your roots to spread out and help the plants multiply. Twelve inches deep is superb." Keep in mind, Mark added, "you want it to be well drained. Daylilies want very well drained soil and do not like to stay wet."

In the absence of rain, which works like magic on daylilies, weekly watering might be necessary during hot periods. Mark advises watering only after 6:00 p.m. from spring until fall. The problem with morning watering is that it keeps the soil moist, and the hot summer sun will result in "boiling your daylilies' shallow roots into soup."

Daylilies are not heavy feeders. He fertilizes his daylilies around Valentine's Day with a slow-release 270-day fertilizer, then follows up in April with an occasional foliar spraying of Miracle-Gro. "Once you see scapes"—leafless flower stalks—"stop foliar spraying," he advised. Incidentally, if you are struck by the fact that nobody is feeding those blooming daylilies growing like weeds along roadsides, the reason might be that they probably have storage-type rhizomes rather than roots typical of today's hybrid daylilies.

After four or five years, daylily roots tend to become overcrowded (matted), resulting in diminished flowering. A decline in flowering, in fact, is a sign that the plants need to be divided. Late fall is the best time for this intervention. Summer is the worst time. Remember not to bury the crowns, which otherwise can rot. And don't hope that daylily roots will thrive while competing with tree roots.

Dormant versus Evergreen

The naturalized daylilies of my childhood had narrow, flat-edged petals; and their colors were limited to solid yellow, orange, or bronze. In contrast, today's cultivars range significantly in height, petal form (flat or crinkled edges), and even floral shade and flower shape (triangular, circular, double, spidery, or star-contoured). Many of these cultivars are tetraploids, and this multiplying of the usual number of chromosomes significantly enhances flower size and hue.

However, selecting a daylily solely on its looks can be a big mistake. It is important to know whether that gorgeous cultivar is evergreen, semievergreen, or dormant. And these three types of daylily can vary even within a marketed series. For instance, the extensive Spacecoast series of daylilies, reported to do well in my Austin area, includes both evergreens and semievergreens.

Dormant daylilies defoliate in winter and require cold temperatures. Dormants vary in how much coldness they require, and unfortunately this information is rarely available.

Semievergreen daylilies retain a very small portion of their foliage after freezes and tend to thrive throughout our state.

Evergreen daylilies retain their foliage all year, and, interestingly, most hybrid evergreens are sufficiently cold-hardy to grow well even in North Texas.

To identify whether a particular daylily cultivar is evergreen, semi-evergreen, or dormant, check the free online database (http://www.daylilies.org/DaylilyDB/) provided by the American Hemerocallis Society (AHS).

While Mark does not recommend dormant daylilies for the southern half of Texas, he has in fact successfully grown at least two—'Red Volunteer' and 'Ruby Spider'—in his San Antonio backyard. Both of these hybrids also scored among the top thirteen most popular day-lilies in one recent AHS poll of Texan and New Mexican gardeners. 'Sweet Patootie,' another dormant, placed eighth in that same survey.

Mark has also had good backyard results with semievergreens 'Moonlit Masquerade' (cream-hued flowers with violet hubs), 'Color Me Happy' (coral-pink flowers with chartreuse throats), and 'Orange Velvet' (tangerine flowers with green centers). 'Color Me Happy' (hybridized by Mary Gage in Cedar Creek, Texas) and 'Moonlight Masquerade' both scored among the top ten in an AHS poll. Other semievergreens scoring among the top nine included (in descending order of popularity) 'Beautiful Edgings,' 'Witches Wink,' and 'Black Ambrosia.' Also over the years excellent results have been reported in our state for sun-yellow 'Bill Norris' and yellow-maroon 'Jason Salter.'

Evergreen daylilies offer Texans "the best chance for floral success," Mark believes. Among the varieties that Mark has grown in his San Antonio backyard and that also "have proven over time to be good performers for the most basic gardener" were two evergreens: peach-hued 'How Beautiful Heaven Must Be' and lavender-petaled 'Cosmic Kaleidoscope.' Both are fragrant hybrids bred by Mark's uncle, Jack Carpenter, at the Lily Farm in Center. 'How Beautiful Heaven Must Be' scored first place and 'Cosmic Kaleidoscope' scored eleventh place in a recent AHS regional survey. Both cultivars, it's also worth noting, are lightly hued. So both are likely to withstand exposure to our intense sunlight. According to the Austin Hemerocallis Society (www.austin-daylily.org), pastel colors (pink, yellow, and orange) do best with six hours of direct morning sun, whereas dark colors (red and purple) do better in the shade.

Prize-winning 'Joan Senior,' an off-white evergreen, has scored well in past AHS surveys for Texas. It displays curved, creped petals with a yellow-tinged throat. The spidery, white-pink and semicrinkled 'Wind Frills' has previously scored even higher, as has luxurious lavender-yellow 'Ida's Braid,' with bright golden ruffles. In a recent Texas/New Mexico AHS poll, evergreens 'Pasty Carpenter,' 'Little Orange Tex,' and 'Ming Porcelain' placed fifth, sixth, and twelfth respectively.

Bearded Irises

Irises are more fleeting than daylilies—"belles of the day" enjoying a "short reign of beauty," according to Thomas Jefferson. Bearded irises were among his favorite flowers. A bearded iris bloom is indeed strikingly elegant: three upright petals (standards) with three arched petals (falls) ornamented by a fuzzy nectar guide. Clearly, Jefferson lamented the transience of this perennial's eye-catching splendor—the fact that bearded irises bloom briefly in early spring.

I suppose there are Texans who consider bearded irises to be ho-hum plants. I don't, especially since I have not given them prime real estate (so to speak). I have many Texas-tough bearded irises that I gratefully received as pass-alongs or that I found growing (apparently for some time) in grass clippings discarded in a nearby field. I value their enduring strappy foliage all year long beneath my live oaks (admittedly not the best place for them), and I think of their spring blooms as nifty bonuses.

Bearded irises are not created equal. Although as a rule they are easy to grow in a wide range of conditions, many perform best in regions with cold winters while others thrive in southern summer heat. So it pays to get the skinny on any bearded iris before buying it.

This is especially true for Texas, where heat, drought, and soil alkalinity can inhibit the short-season, cooler-weather irises commonly marketed. For home landscapes unable to support our state's moisture-loving wild irises—zigzag iris (*Iris brevicaulis*), giant blue iris

(*I. giganticaerulea*), yellow flag (*I. pseudacorus*), and southern blue flag (*I. virginica*)—we need Texas-tough alternatives. The good news is that local hybridizers are producing them.

Extending Their Reign

How delighted Jefferson would have been to hear of repeat-blooming irises. Today, in fact, getting one-time bloomers to reflower has emerged as a horticultural frontier, which now includes even new varieties of hydrangeas and lilacs.

Several years ago Renée Shearer gave me a crash-course introduction to reblooming (remontant) bearded irises. She had lived in Austin for twenty-five years before starting an iris business in Decatur in 2002. At that time she was a self-confessed iris addict with an insatiable hunger, she recalled, "for growing them, reading about them, visiting nurseries to see them, and pinching starts from people"—friends and strangers alike. "Rural life in Decatur was wonderful," Renée recalled, but personal circumstances required her to move to Waco and then to haul her irises in 2005 to Odessa, where she founded Wild Prairie Farm.

Unfortunately, Renée has closed the iris farm. For years she promoted the farm heavily, gave educational presentations year-round, and physically managed everything alone while "evolving as a pottery artist." When she had the opportunity to follow her "true passion," she sold off her remaining remontant stock to different growers, but kept enough in the ground to restart the business if she so desired and to fill any unsolicited orders that came in.

From what I have seen with plant addictions, it would not be a sure thing to bet that Renée has permanently broken free and clear of the hold that irises have previously had on her for so long. Only time will tell.

Renée had been featuring iris selections developed by Texan hybridizers, including Tom Burseen in Grand Prairie and Vincent Christopherson at Accent Iris Garden in Arlington. She proudly spoke of her remontants as "Texas-tough beauties born and bred in harsh growing conditions." Irises capable of thriving in the "worst soil conditions of West Texas," she believed, could grow just about anywhere.

Renée's repeat-iris lessons are as enduring as pass-along plants exchanged among friends over many years. And I'm passing on those lessons here.

Reflowering irises bloom in the spring and then sometimes also in the fall. How often they flower varies based on their treatment and local conditions. Rebloomers inspire hope in a second show but come with no guarantee. "Each has its own character and will rebloom when it wants to," Renée told me.

Basically, remontant irises require the same amount of care as do the more common tall bearded irises: excellent drainage in neutral to slightly alkaline soil exposed daily to at least five hours of sunlight. Excessive heat and dryness can impede iris flowering generally, but such conditions especially inhibit a rebloomer's replay. Remontants must not go dormant due to protracted dryness, Renée advised, adding that drip irrigation is ideal for them. Repeat-blooming irises tend to need more water than more typical bearded selections and also extra feedings with a low-nitrogen, high-phosphorus fertilizer, such as 5-10-5. Renée recommended feeding them on Valentine's Day, Memorial Day, Labor Day, and Halloween.

There is a good reason why rebloomers need more water and nourishment. All bearded irises sprout leaf fans from thick underground stems (rhizomes). Usually it takes an entire year for an iris rhizome to produce a new bud and a flower stalk. Instead of one year, though, remontant irises complete this new growth cycle in one season. That's their distinctive difference, Renée pointed out.

Individual varieties of bearded iris, including the remontants, commonly vary in their performance depending on their setting. In contrast to time-tested Texas iris pass-alongs, many of the elaborate and appealing iris hybrids available in plant nursery catalogs or sold in local box stores benefit from cold winters and mild summers. When planted in Texas, these rhizomes might flower for one or maybe two years, but then they often dwindle away. Generally, as advised by Joe and Donna Spears when they operated Argyle Acres Iris Gardens, "in Texas, bearded irises grow best north and west of US 59—between Houston and Laredo. They require a definite winter season not found farther south or near the Gulf Coast."

Being able to avoid guessing which irises will perform in our state was one reason why "Texas-tough" iris hybrids have been such a boon. For those of us unable to grow our state's moisture-loving wild irises, some iris-selection guidance can be useful. I have found that various

Texas-based iris societies are often extremely helpful when identifying which cultivars have performed well in their vicinities. Members of the Iris Society of Austin, for instance, pointed to 'Cantina,' 'Fall Spotlight,' 'Eleanor Roosevelt,' 'Holy Kosmoly,' and especially 'Daughter of Stars' as reblooming successes, though even these can be variable.

Troubleshooting

So far, my rebloomers have flowered beautifully each year, but they have never repeated. I blame myself. I'm neglectful, a "halfway iris-keeper" whose yard too often displays plenty of evergreen bearded iris leaf fans but precious few flowers. I have even convinced myself, as I stated earlier in this book, that I just love those iris fans. After all, they are so durable despite the local weather and my neglect.

I know I should divide and replant my crowded rhizomes. And sometimes I do. But a year-round punishing lack of rain in my region often puts unwelcome finishing touches on my best efforts. I water them with conserved rainwater, at least for as long as my too-soon-depleted reserves last. Relying on tap water that hasn't been stored for a day before use unfortunately contributes chemicals detrimental to plant performance. In my case, too, tap water reinforces the alkalinity of my soil.

Which brings me to a phenomenon reported by some iris-keepers—a peculiarity concerning iris hue that I have witnessed in a neighbor's yard.

A good example of this phenomenon is described in a letter printed in an issue of *Texas Gardener*. "I have had a strange thing this year," Betty Johnson wrote concerning her formerly peachy-pink 'Happy Birthday' irises. "As the years have gone by . . . the color has lightened until they have been a sand color for a few years, until this year when the top-level bed bloomed a perfectly snow-white."

A common explanation for this phenomenon is that white iris is an extremely aggressive rhizome that can invade and take over a bed. Appeasing my skepticism, I have searched for and so far failed to find botanic confirmation of this widely held view of rampant white irises. The notion might be true; I just can't confirm it scientifically.

I have found something else, though, that more likely pertains to the phenomenon. A clue, I think, lies in Betty's suggestion of a hue-fading or bleaching sequence over time: peachy-pink becoming sand-hued in turn becoming whitish. She reports "a perfectly snow-white" stage, but I wonder if, considered upclose, those flowers aren't actually a pale off-white.

It is genetically impossible for irises to change color, but their capacity to express their color can be compromised. The successful floral expression of color requires certain levels of acidity in the petal cells. "Even mild shifts in acidity may alter their absorbance and color properties," David Lee has explained in *Nature's Palette*.

Besides acidity level, various chemical compounds (coenzymes) in petal cell sap play an even bigger role in the expression of color. These coenzymes, Fritz Köhlein observed in *Iris*, can be impeded by one or more mineral deficiencies or by an excess of some mineral(s). So soil environment is important generally to successful iris flowering and specifically to the expression of iris floral color. It is good to keep in mind, for instance, that bearded irises (in contrast to Siberian and Japanese irises) prefer a slightly alkaline to neutral soil pH, but much of Texas is way more alkaline than "slightly."

The hue-fading or bleaching sequence of Betty Johnson's irises over time suggests not a change in their color but, instead, their increasing inability to express their color. Of course, I turned to Renée for some insight.

She had heard of "the bleaching issue," though only from some of her southern customers. She recommended refreshing the iris bed's soil nutrients, which probably have become depleted due to the overcrowding. She added: "Fluff up the bed with compost and organic matter and water once a week when there is no rain."

Reluctant to let Renée return to her gorgeous pottery, I wheedled for just one more insider tip about remontant irises. And then she revealed a secret practice she admitted is controversial. Renée mulches her irises with layered newspaper and bark—in Decatur she used hay—to within four to six inches of each rhizome. This newspaper mulch, she told me, retains moisture, controls weeds, and decomposes/composts over time.

"It's all good!" Renée told me about the multiple benefits of her mulching technique. But her comment expresses much more. It conveys the passion she can still feel as an iris-lover spellbound by the bright, colorful, "all-good" wonderland of the rebloomers.

20

Buckwheat to the Rescue

I met Tony Roca at a meeting of the Fredericksburg Area Beekeepers at the Gillespie County Extension Office. He has transformed about five (out of ten) drought-stricken acres of former ranchland in Harper into a habitat that so far is sustaining ten thriving bee colonies. Tony is following the standard prescribed by the agricultural land-use guidelines established for the state of Texas, which limits beekeeping to between five and twenty acres, with a required minimum of six colonies on five acres.

Bee Islands

Tony is an impressive can-do person who even constructed a huge rake designed to clear his land with a minimum of scraping. He removed dead, fallen, and dying oaks from the Harper acreage and then attached the homemade rake to a bulldozer to get rid of cacti, yuccas, greenbriar, thistles, sandburs, bindweed, and buffalo burs, among many other Hill Country nuisance plants. This effort resulted in a relatively tidied-up and certainly more manageable landscape dotted with a few remaining drought-stressed but (hopefully) viable trees.

The rake was also designed to lightly disturb the soil surface of Tony's property. This undertaking fostered a welcome abundance of wildflowers whose seeds (previously buried beneath decaying ranchscape debris) finally got to see the light of day one spring. Both outcomes were total plusses for Tony as well as for his "bee islands," as he refers to the apian colonies located in dappled settings beneath the saved trees on his land.

The unexpected wildflowers were good news for as long as they

Tony Roca's beehives in Harper

Bee raiding buckwheat

lasted. But desiccating drought was still miserably rampant in the Hill Country, and drought is inimical to flowering native plants and likewise to bee-colony health and endurance. During long periods of heat and dryness, Tony noted, "there's not much for bees to forage or even many bees available to work the fields because they are busy cooling the hive." Weather is a recurrent concern: he said he was constantly reminded that farming—whether bees, crops, or livestock—includes "a never-ending awareness of how little you know, and every problem is a chance to learn a little more."

So Tony began to consider creating an open space to be covered with a flowering crop that would compensate for long periods when wildflowers were absent from his rain-parched locale. In late August 2013 he cleared a third of an acre and planted buckwheat, a tried-and-true, nectar-rich bee magnet that contributes to a uniquely flavored dark honey. In later years he would also plant several pounds of wildflower seed.

"Mancan" Buckwheat

There are not many varieties of buckwheat readily available in US markets. An unclassified type (simply labeled "buckwheat" and indeterminate in its genetic consistency) is fairly common at farm-supply outlets. Tony, however, selected 'Mancan,' which he ordered through Behrends, a local feedstore in Harper.

"When I looked around for seeds, I found several varieties and sources, some nearly three dollars a pound—I think from sources catering to 'boutique' growers," Tony recalled. "I was able to get 'Mancan' for about one dollar a pound in fifty-pound bags, which was as much as I was willing to pay for this first level of my experiment."

'Mancan' is a newer cultivar developed by Agriculture Canada and has become a prominent choice for buckwheat growers in the southeastern states of our country. 'Mancan' is more vigorous than older buckwheat cultivars, such as 'Tempest' and 'Tokyo.' And this newer mid-season buckwheat potentially yields larger leaves, stems, and seeds.

Tony's land has good soil, enriched by years of ranching. Even so, sunlight-loving buckwheat is easy to grow in poor soil, too, as long as its drainage is excellent. And buckwheat is a short-season crop. It grows rapidly, tending to bear flowers within four to six weeks after germinating from seeds planted less than an inch deep. After that, at least in

Tony's late-summer/early-autumn experience in Harper, buckwheat blooms prolifically for two weeks on ten- to twelve-inch plants before going to seed. In less droughty and heat-saturated environments than Texas, buckwheat plants can grow taller (between two and four feet high), and their bloom period tends to be a few weeks longer.

There is more good news about buckwheat as a pollinator-sustainer: it thrives without deep watering. In fact, lingering wetness will kill it. It has a strong, though slender, moisture-retaining taproot that enables the plant to endure dry conditions. So while Hill Country water resources remained limited, Tony had to wet only the surface ground of his buckwheat crop about once a week.

Whereas this plant's moisture-conserving taproot might grow as deep as ten inches in more favorable climatic conditions, Tony's plants achieved only two- to three-inch taproots. Still, that size proved to be ample enough to sustain his plants. In his experience, most of buckwheat's dense, fibrous, superficial root system stayed close to the top of the soil, making light (surface-only) maintenance watering sufficiently effective.

Smother/Cover Crop

Buckwheat is not a grain, but actually a rhubarb or sorrel relative classified as a pseudocereal. For some of us, the mention of buckwheat might stir memories of morning groats (porridge) and pioneer-type pancakes. For others, this plant might appeal because it is a source of gluten-free food, including buckwheat noodles (soba) and a type of beer.

Such thoughts, however, are not likely to advance the case for buckwheat as a top choice to ornament home landscapes. It's pretty, in my opinion, and its cute, mostly-white flowers are fragrant. Even so, buckwheat plants tend to remain small in most of Texas and do not quite escape an agricultural look. Nor will home-milling buckwheat seed be a likely payoff, either, because removing the outer hull of its triangular-shaped seed requires special equipment.

If for some gardeners buckwheat might not seem to be the most appealing addition to a garden bed, it is nonetheless by far preferable when compared with the opportunistic and irksome weeds that commonly pop up in disturbed beds not presently under active cultivation. In fact, fast-growing buckwheat has a strong reputation as a "smother crop" because it readily suppresses and displaces weeds.

And there is still another way to think about this plant. Buckwheat the smother crop also makes an excellent cover crop. So besides being a boon to local honey and native bees that need all the help they can get at present, buckwheat can be used to revitalize a "tired" garden bed. It is not a nitrogen-fixer (such as clover, cowpea, and peanut), but buckwheat adds organic richness to the earth when turned under as a "green manure."

Among other benefits, buckwheat can take up insoluble phosphorus, which in that form remains unavailable to most plants. When spent buckwheat plants are hoed into the soil, they decompose and then refund this captured phosphorous in a form now easily accessed by other plants grown later in that same garden bed. Phosphorus (P), the middle number of the three listed on plant fertilizers, is critical to root development, photosynthesis, and both flower and seed proliferation.

Seed Foraging

In some garden beds reseeding can be an issue with buckwheat, though such stray rebounders can be simply pulled up. Tony, of course, is glad if his crop reseeds—between twelve to twenty seeds per plant, he estimates. He managed to harvest "a lot of seeds and only did so after the second frost." The seeds "must be dry and mature before attempting to harvest them," he advises.

Eventually, deer foraged what buckwheat seeds remained after Tony's harvest. Actually, he was lucky in that regard. Elsewhere in Texas, beekeepers report considerable and much earlier buckwheat loss to deer raids. Tony wondered whether the deer in his vicinity "might now have an acquired taste for this 'new' food source." If so, he is typically prepared: "We have a deer fence we would put up if we decide to grow buckwheat before or after the wildflowers bloom."

Sometimes, indeed, good fences make good neighbors. Sometimes, though, fences are not enough. It is very likely that some avian denizens of Harper took their seed-share of Tony's original buckwheat bounty—possibly while his back was turned. Buckwheat appeals to birds as well as other pollinators (especially butterflies), and it is an ingredient in some commercial birdseed. So whether or not the deer come calling again—perhaps sooner rather than later next time—the pirating birds will be back, for sure.

21

Orchids for Everyone

There are so many misconceptions about orchids it's hard to know where to start with the facts. This is not a recent problem. Throughout human history, the exotic—some would say, provocative—appearance of orchids has inspired peculiar notions.

At the top of the list, perhaps, is the ancient belief that certain orchids are aphrodisiacs. Madness of a different order seems to have afflicted people who risked everything, even their lives, to possess one or another orchid. Their stories are documented in Susan Orlean's *The Orchid Thief*, Eric Hansen's *Orchid Fever*, and Luigi Berliocchi's *The Orchid in Lore and Legend*.

My childhood introduction to orchid obsession was "The Flowering of the Strange Orchid," an 1894 short story by H. G. Wells. It's about an orchid with "tentacle-like aerial rootlets" and "leech-like suckers" seeking human blood. Today this story is usually read as a horror tale, but in its time it was also understood as a satire on the orchid craze that had besieged England during Wells's youth. That was a period when the lucrative demand for and reputations associated with unusual orchids sent Victorian plant hunters on frenzied, perilous searches across the globe.

Wells, I imagine, would have appreciated the creation, in 1978, of the *Dracula* genus for over 100 "little dragon" orchids native to Central America. This group, with flowers sometimes appearing blood-splattered or blood-streaked, includes the ominously named *Dracula vampira*.

Misconceptions about orchids frequently include distortions of basic facts. The flamboyant appearance of the most commercialized orchids suggests to some that these plants are rare or that they come only from distant places. Of course, there are rare and endangered orchids, and the showiest of the group—the ones we dote on—do hale from exotic places. Even so, as a plant group, there are tens of thousands of orchid species spread worldwide. Orchids, in fact, likely comprise as much of 10 percent of all flowering plants.

There are quite a number of native orchids in the United States. My first viewing of a wild orchid was a yellow lady's-slipper, a protected plant spotted during a 1960s botany-class field trip in New Jersey. Texas has its share, too, as documented in Joe and Ann Orto Liggio's beautiful *Wild Orchids of Texas*. Most Texas orchids are not common in the wild, and many are under increasing stress from habitat attrition. There is no commercial interest in native Texas orchids, mainly because they are difficult to transplant and each species has special habitat requirements hard to duplicate at home.

Uprooting Orchid Fear

Mistaken impressions about rareness or distant origins are hardly the only or even the most prevalent misconceptions about orchids. Imagined difficulties with growing them at home are far more common, Geoffrey Frost has remarked. He lives with more than 300 orchids acquired over a decade of collecting in Austin, where he has served as president of the Heart O' Texas Orchid Society and has garnered several American Orchid Society merit awards. Besides serving as show chairperson at the Heart O' Texas Orchid Society, he has also been a representative for the American Orchid Society and for the SouthWest Regional Orchid Growers Association.

Geoffrey loves to take the chill out of people's fear of growing orchids. Start, he suggested, by uprooting a common misperception about orchids—that they are very delicate. "They may look that way, but in fact they are very hardy, with some plants blooming for several months." Growing orchids at home is not difficult, Geoffrey explained. "In some ways, it is easier than most common houseplants." Orchids, in fact, "can take much more neglect than one would think," though of course cared-for plants perform better.

Even so, Juanice Davis advised, there is one caution to keep in mind when considering a purchase: "Don't be tempted by the flowers." As someone who for years specialized in orchids and roses in Austin, Juanice insisted that paying attention to growing requirements should overrule the lure of bewitching beauty, "unless you just want the flowers and don't intend to grow the plant."

Her point is that orchids differ in their needs, some being fussier than others. So, I asked, what would be the best orchids for beginners—orchids anyone can grow?

Rooting for Moth Orchids

Geoffrey and Juanice concurred that *Phalaenopsis* orchids are the best gateway type, which probably explains why these so-called moth orchids are the most common type sold at garden centers, big-box outlets, and even grocery stores. "They grow well at home with minimal light and enjoy the same temperatures that we do," Geoffrey explained. Another plus, Juanice added, is that they "retain their blooms at least two months, sometimes more if they receive proper care."

White Phalaenopsis

Since *Phalaenopsis* includes sixty or so species and many hybrids, not all of them have precisely the same requirements. The six- to eight-inch miniatures of this group, for example, might seem somewhat easier to accommodate as a houseplant, but actually they are the hardest of the *Phalaenopsis* genus to manage because they tend to require drier and cooler conditions. "Some miniatures also have high light requirements," Juanice noted. "And remember, too," Geoffrey advised, "the smaller the pot, the quicker it dries out. With miniatures, it's best to check with local orchid businesses to determine which ones are likely to thrive in your home."

Before purchasing an orchid, "be sure to look the plant over well, both under and on top of the leaves, for any sign of pest or disease," Geoffrey recommended. "The leaves should be a medium green and the roots should be firm to the touch and not mushy. Also check the medium in which the orchid is planted to make sure it is not too soggy or rotted."

Care of Moth Orchids

To keep any home orchid healthy, consult the detailed care sheets available from the American Orchid Society. There is, though, such a thing as "overcare," Juanice warned, resulting in a plant standing in water, positioned beneath an air vent, or situated in too large a pot. "The biggest killer of moth orchids is overwatering," Geoffrey said. "People tend to think that most orchids are tropical in nature and need lots of water, but the opposite is true for *Phalaenopsis*. Orchids attach themselves to trees in the wild, and when it rains they are able to absorb water rather quickly and then dry out before the next rainfall. But potted orchids take a few days to totally dry out, and so less water is better for them."

There are several factors that do warrant concern. One is providing *Phalaenopsis* with sufficient sunlight. Not direct sunlight, Juanice stressed, but six or more hours of diffused or filtered light, such as a brightly lit, untinted east window. "Keeping your *Phalaenopsis* cool is a must in our Texas heat," Geoffrey explained. "Temperatures over 95 degrees will start to cook the plant. Orchids are like people when it comes to temperatures and humidity. If you're comfortable, then your orchids are comfortable. If you're cold or hot, then you can bet your orchids are, too."

Phalaenopsis hybrid

Often extra humidity helps, according to Geoffrey. "This can be done by filling a tray with small pebbles or stones and then barely covering the top of the pebbles with water. Place the orchid pot on the top of the stones but not directly in the water. This will help produce extra humidity around the plants. As the water in the tray evaporates, place more water in the tray." And, Juanice suggested, it's a good idea to provide some air circulation with ceiling fans.

Since a *Phalaenopsis* has no water-storing capability, it is important to never allow these orchids to dry out completely between waterings. "They like to stay somewhat moist at all times," Geoffrey said. When nearly dry, water them thoroughly. It helps to invest in an inexpensive water meter.

Juanice and Geoffrey agree that repotting every two years or so is a good plan because over time the orchid's potting medium degrades, to the detriment of the plant.

A *Phalaenopsis* should be fed regularly, especially during warm weather when the plant is most active. "Give the orchid a little bit of water-soluble fertilizer once or twice a month," Geoffrey indicated. "Just make sure you dilute the fertilizer one-fourth to one-half the strength of what is called for on the package." He says any brand will do, and he usually buys whatever is on sale. Juanice cautioned against time-release fertilizers because our Lone Star heat can fatally accelerate the nutrient-release rate. "Time-release fertilizer is used for orchids in Hawaii and other places cooler than Texas," she reported, "but when I tried it on an entire tray of orchids, the roots burned and I lost every plant."

Horrid Unruly Roots

Geoffrey also tells a "horror" story about orchid roots. A woman once telephoned him for help in saving her orchids. They had performed well for some time, and she was watering them properly, but now they were drying up and dying. "I asked if she was doing anything different," Geoffrey remembered, "and she said no, except for cutting away the runners—those long things that come off the plants and hang out of the pots—because they're so ugly." Runners? Frost wondered for a moment before realizing what she meant. He told her to stop cutting her orchids' roots.

Orchids are epiphytes, nonparasitic plants that attach themselves to other flora solely for support. Without these supporting roots, an orchid is less able to take up water and nutrients.

The woman's ugly roots were easier to manage than Wells's fictional vampiric ones. "If you don't like the way the roots look growing outside the pot," Geoffrey told her, "just plant them in a larger pot so the roots have somewhere to grow." He advised a new container one size bigger than the old one, but cautioned, "just be careful not to damage the roots when transplanting."

Maybe, too, another caution is in order—something Juanice referred to as the potato-chip effect: "If you buy one orchid, you will want another or 50 more." That's what happened to her, not that she's complaining.

In Geoffrey's case, all it took was merely seeing a friend's gorgeous house-raised *Phalaenopsis* with large white flowers spread as wide as moth wings. "Well, that did it for me," he recalled. "I had just been bitten by the orchid bug, and my life would never be the same again. I started with one, then two, then ten—I just couldn't get enough, even after running out of room again and again, and now it's over 300 orchids later!"

22

High-Voltage Violets

If my own thoughts were typical, it's easy to have misconceptions about African violets. It would be a mistake, though, to believe that these fuzzy-leafed tropicals are too finicky to be endured or that they are doted on only by Mayberryish Aunt Beas.

I had my eyes opened at several African violet shows. There are many such shows, often listed on websites for the Lone Star African Violet Council and the African Violet Society of America. During my visits to these exhibitions and markets, I was struck by the range of juried entries. It was impressive to see them all, but they made me wonder just what qualifies for an African violet show.

African Violets and More

So I turned to three people who would know: Anne Nicholas in Denton, Marge Savage in Midland, and Penny Smith-Kerker in Austin. Each oversees an extensive collection of African violets (including their own award-winning entries), and each has a long association (often including various official duties) with their regional groups, the statewide Lone Star African Violet Council, and also the national African Violet Society of America.

"Just what qualifies for an African violet show?" I asked. "That's a great question," Anne cheerfully and patiently started, preparing to ease me gently off the hook of my naïveté.

She explained that the African violets (*Saintpaulia*) seen in supermarkets or on kitchen windowsills actually belong to a much larger family of plants called gesneriads (*Gesneriaceae*). "The shows contain lots of African violets plus their cousins, the other gesneriads, includ-

'Mac's Fiery Fascination' Saintpaulia

ing *Streptocarpus, Episcias, Chiritas, Sinningias, Columneas,* and many others. In a judged show," Anne continued, "African violets and the other gesneriads are evaluated in separate categories. There are awards for both the best African violets and for the best other gesneriads."

African violets and the other gesneriads are not just cousins, Penny added. "Care is very similar for most of them; so almost all the club members grow at least a few other gesneriads with their African violets." They are simply too irresistible to ignore, she suggested. "There are so *many* different gesneriads that it's fun growing them for their unique blossoms as well as for their variations in leaf shapes, sizes, veining, and color."

Okay, then, an African violet show is really a gesneriad show, though the general public might be clueless if it were actually billed as such. And it turns out, too, that even the popular *Saintpaulia* species, for which the African violet shows are named, are actually gloxinia relatives, not violets at all.

But, of course, I have more questions. I have noticed about a half-dozen African violets on a north-facing windowsill of Veggie Heaven, a unique restaurant once located across from the University of Texas campus in Austin. There they sat flowering year-round at room temperature, in parking-lot light, and with seemingly minimal attention, and I always thought: can their care be that easy?

The answer, apparently, is mostly "yes" and a little "no." Setting up is easy enough—a healthy plant, a pot, a saucer, and both African violet soil and food. Although there are specialty pots designed specifically for African violets, "a four-inch, squatty plastic azalea pot works well in Texas," Marge said, "with terracotta and decorative pots used as cache containers for display." The pot sits on a saucer filled with pebbles. Florescent "cool whites" or Gro-Lights (with instructions about distances) are a possibility, but for most of Texas an east or (less ideally) a north windowsill will serve at typical room temperature (around 70 degrees F).

"If you are hot, your violets are too hot," Marge pointed out. "If you are cold, they are too cold. Gently hold a leaf between thumb and forefinger. If it feels warm, then it is too hot. Yes, you can touch them—no nails, please." Since touching causes violet leaves to blacken, Penny humorously speculated, this might be why "your mom told you to keep away from her plants."

Also according to Marge, who cares for over 100 gesneriads in a bedroom (aka "The Plant Room") in dry West Texas, "the biggest misconception about raising African violets or other gesneriads is: 'Oh, I can't grow those,' even though the same doubters might say 'my grandmother used to grow them when . . .' Well, 'Yes, you can!'" she insisted. All it takes is confidence and consistency. "There are easy things you can do. Reading the directions is part of it. We all hate that. Some people have a natural gift for growing and don't need directions; but most of us do."

Which brings us to the "too muches" and the "not enoughs"—about which Penny joked, "It really helps to have mild OCD." But she cares for over 300 plants, all grown under fluorescent lights covering ninety-two square feet of tiered shelving and other surfaces in her home. It took her ten years to get into this situation; so a beginner should be safe for a while.

Elaborate dish display at an African violet show

As for the "too muches" and "not enoughs," gesneriads go bad when underwatered or (even worse) overwatered. "These are fibrous-rooted plants," Marge indicated. "They don't have taproots for water storage. Fertilized water needs to flow through the roots." Experts recommend bottled water or tap water left to stand a day at the plant-room temperature to allow for a reduction of leaf-burning chlorine. In West Texas, Marge told me, many people use reverse osmosis water because of the salt in city water. Cold water results in leaf curling, and wet crowns are prone to rot. Hydrate until the water exits the pot. Discard that dirty water and then, using clean water, barely cover the pebbles on which the pot will sit for humidification without any further direct contact with water.

Secrets of Violet Care

The African Violet Society of America also recommends "wicking"—connecting the saucer and the bottom of the pot with moisture-conductive two-ply nylon yarn, four-ply acrylic baby yard, nylon seining twine, or pantyhose. Marge's African violets are wick-watered. "Small violets and leaves I'm starting are in a plastic tray filled with capillary matting—an old nylon blanket, cut up. I pour the fertilized water in and the blanket takes it up."

There are variations on this theme for her other gesneriads. "I use glass 'bubble' bowls for my episcias, with a huge eighteen-inch one for my terrarium. Mini sinningias are in small glass bowls. These can come from hobby stores (40 percent off) or garage sales or Goodwill. The glass bowls have a square of Saran Wrap sealing them." Marge also uses a humidifier and vaporizers bought at garage sales. Often she covers her newly potted and stressed plants with a clear plastic bag. "Humidity cures lots of things," she assured me. "I have plastic domes that fit the trays for my leaf propagation. Without the domes in our dry climate, the plants really don't put up 'babies' well."

In such settings with low humidity, light spray-misting can be helpful, though gravel-level lukewarm water in the pot's saucer is usually sufficient. "My plants love the mister," Marge noted, but she "waits until the lights go out. Light magnifies through droplets and makes permanent white spots on the leaves. Sunlight will burn them."

Marge's double "ranch windows" in the plant room are blocked off by plasterboard so she can control the fluorescent lighting. When using natural light and windowsills, Marge cautioned, "Remember, the sun is at different heights throughout the seasons. I burned the tar out of some plants on my dining room windowsill because of this. I needed a sheer curtain. When I'm growing for a show, I tape tissue paper to that window. In West Texas northern window exposure is good; eastern is good; southern is best; western is a no-no—too doggone hot!"

If not relying on artificial lightening in Central Texas, Penny advised, "don't let African violets get direct western or southern light, which will burn the leaves." Although these plants do need a lot of light to bloom—for example, her plants get an average of twelve hours of light a day on their stands—the light should be indirect, filtered by a sheer curtain, or direct through a north or east window.

Too much light or nitrogen, the presence of any natural gas, and inadequate darkness (eight hours are needed daily) curtail flowering. Too much dryness or fertilization browns leaf tips and edges. Too much light damages foliage and can stunt growth. Not enough light or humidity also damages foliage.

"Many beginners take the plant home from the mega-market, repot it in a six-inch cache ceramic pot, and fill it with heavy potting soil they bought on sale," Marge observed. "Then the plant goes into shock. It didn't get to go to post-op"—her vivid metaphor for the process of acclimating to the new owner's environment. "Now the plant can't take up water; the roots are fine, but the soil is like clay—so the owner waters it again. The roots rot, and the owner waters it again. The crown rots and so do the lovely blossoms—the reason it was bought in the first place. If the beleaguered plant makes it past this point, the owner wonders why it won't bloom. It won't bloom until all those roots *fill up* the entire six-inch pot they were put in. Otherwise, these plants bloom year-round at six-week intervals. They do better in spring and fall, but they do bloom year-round."

African violets perform best when root-bound, Penny explained, and "if their pot is too large, excessive moisture around the roots will end up rotting the plants." So her secrets for success include using a pot only about one-third of the plant's diameter, repotting annually, and (when necessary) increasing container size by increments of one-half to one inch. For every hydration (except once-a-month plain watering), she adds African violet fertilizer at a rate of one-fourth the amount specified on label.

Gesneriad pros are always on the lookout for a variety of diseases and infestations, particularly whenever adding a plant to their collections (for help in diagnosing problems with African violets, visit http://www.avsa.org/learning). Isolate and observe for some time, they recommend, and then study that new plant closely some more. Deadheading spent blooms and also pruning damaged foliage are crucial to plant-disease prevention, not to mention the maintenance of beauty.

Violet Emotions

Such vigilance yields rich rewards, and not just lush flowering plants. Penny might joke about being obsessive-compulsive over her fuzzy-leafed charges, yet she also speaks glowingly about her time with them. "Generally, I find it very calming and relaxing to work with my plants. I always tell my family, which includes two boys, that I'm going to 'play with my plants.' My African violets don't talk back, don't ask for money or the car keys, and when they really aggravate me, I can just throw them out!"

Sometimes that can be easier said than done, Marge acknowledged. "These are my babies. The first time I suspected I had a 'bug,' I was literally sick! I ran for my Sunset guidebook *How to Grow African Violets* and, yes, my plant was sick!" Now, what to do, she worried. It was her first and favorite African violet—an 'Optimara Trinidad' with lovely white-edged lavender flowers. "I took it outside and doused the mealy-bug-infected top and root ball in malathion. It smelled so bad that I left it on the warm, shaded front porch to drip dry. But I forgot it overnight when the temperature fell below 55 degrees F. By morning my favorite plant was gone, and I was crushed."

That's not the end of the story, though. Marge clipped and rinsed between twelve and eighteen leaves that seemed to be still alive, and she put them in plastic bags for warmth. Later she potted each one in a 2½-inch pot filled with vermiculite (for West Texas). "They all made it," she remembered, "resulting in many 'babies' that were given away, sold at plant sales, or kept."

While "some people would have tossed a sick plant into a Dumpster," Marge admitted, "not me! I always try to bring it back. That's where you learn great lessons! Some growers feel as if letting one go is like killing someone. When separating the many new babies from one 'mother leaf' to make new plants, some growers *cannot* throw any extras away. We are creating! There is something visceral about it."

Maybe that's how Anne has arrived at the 500 violets creating "a wonderful oxygen-rich environment" in both a guest and a master bedroom in Denton. She finds that "after a long day of work, spending a little time potting or grooming the plants can be very relaxing. African violets respond to care with new growth and more blooms—almost as if they are grateful."

For Anne, sometimes memories are involved, especially of her childhood on a farm outside Waxahachie, where she loved playing in dirt. There are other kinds of memories as well: "One of my husband's hybrids is 'Lonestar Helen Mahr,' named after his mother. So, often, when we are working with our violets, we not only enjoy the relaxing process of potting, but we also think of events and special folks in our lives."

Violet Tales

Calmness, relaxation, and welcome memories are ideal experiences. Even so, gesneriad pros do relate darker tales, too. New York hybridizer Dr. Ralph Robinson, Anne recalled, named one of his new hybrids 'Rob's Suicidal Squirrel,' recalling a squirrel that ran in front of his car while he was driving to an African violet show.

Mortality can also haunt the plant room. "I've killed many plants, probably hundreds by now," Penny confessed. "With gesneriads being so easy to propagate, I don't worry or even try to keep every one anymore."

Even so, sometimes Penny's efforts to enhance their lives have complicated her life. "When I was new to African violets and forum participants were raving about how great fish fertilizer was for their plants, I tried it. I let the plants absorb the treated water in large trays, and everything seemed fine that night," Penny recalled. "But when I got home the next day after work, the whole house smelled like rotten fish. I had to remove the plants and drag all the trays outside to be thoroughly washed. What a mess! This was probably the most embarrassing thing I ever did with my plants."

Anne admitted her own misadventures with gesneriads and particularly lamented an incident with one of her husband's African violets. They were living in San Antonio at the time and planned a trip to a state show in Austin, where for the first time Richard would enter some of his plants in the competition. She remembers that this decision "was a very big deal!"

Richard was especially proud of a profusely blooming 'Pink Energy' African violet, which measured an extraordinary thirty-two inches across with "incredible symmetry—a perfect circle of leaves—one of the most important criteria counted by the judges of a show." Anne was being careful—she really was—as she tilted the enormous plant to get it through the doorway to the car, but the plant slipped and was damaged when she scrambled to catch it. What once was a symmetrical tropical now was half-moon-shaped. "I could not believe what I had done!" she recalled. "Needless to say, that rather silent trip to Austin had one plant missing."

Violets and Gender

Anne's marriage survived, and their African violet partnership also remained intact. Actually, there's a little backstory to their joint gesneriad venture. "Richard had always loved his grandmother's violets," Anne reminisced, and so she wasn't completely surprised when he purchased an African violet ('Ballet Lisa') at a mall show in Austin to give her on their first wedding anniversary. It wasn't long, though, before Richard was caring for their first African violet, and many years later he would even release five hybrids in his 'Lonestar' African violet series.

Clearly, men are fascinated by African violets and will get their hands on them one way or another. Even so, these tropicals are often perceived as girly plants. Half-seriously, I asked Anne if she thought there was a gender gap among African violet growers.

"I think that African violets are often perceived as girly because of their names," Anne admitted. "Violets with names such as 'Red Velvet,' 'Jolly Snow White,' or 'Buckeye Love's Caress' suggest the more feminine qualities of beauty, colors, or sentimental feelings." And it is true, she added, that "the earliest violet clubs emerged from the predominantly female garden clubs." But that was long ago, Anne pointed out, "and today many of the best growers and hybridizers in the United States are men." Anne rattled off an impressive list of men currently involved in the field, including "an ex-military Texan who rides a Harley-Davidson, raises horses, and creates the teeny-tiniest floral designs with African violets."

Asked and answered, then, with nothing going sideways. It is evident, too, that being male or female makes no difference in how owning one little African violet will likely lead to the acquisition of other gesneriads. One of these tropicals is rarely enough and invites further plant and human connections. "You can be involved with growers all over the world," Penny said. "It really is amazing. I've traded leaves with people all over the United States and from South Africa."

Violet Addiction

If growing African violets is much easier than most people tend to imagine, so is getting addicted to them. For Marge, maybe it all started with her mom: "I first became interested in the Queen of Houseplants when my mother brought them into the house. It was after World War II, and people turned to more pleasant pastimes instead of saving tinfoil for the scrap metal drive and putting your favorite rubber dolly into the war effort. I'm sure my mother grew nearly all the original ten Armacost & Royston hybrids: 'Blue Boy,' 'Pink Girl,' 'Admiral,' 'Neptune,' and others."

As an adult, Marge occasionally purchased a violet and eventually lost it. One day during retirement, though, she spotted a cart of African violets marked down in a post–Mother's Day sale. "'Take me home,' they cried! So I did. Then I said to myself, 'Self, you're going to keep these plants alive this time!' So I bought *How to Grow African Violets*, read it, and highlighted passages for ready reference."

That's how Marge's violet addiction began. For Anne, all it took was a stealth gift from her husband, and in Penny's case it was a casual, innocent visit to an African violet show in Austin. "I bought a few plants at this show, eventually collected ten to fifteen plants, and got a very small plant stand. But then I had my two boys, got really busy, and managed to keep only one of those original plants. Fifteen years or so later, my sister in Chicago got very interested in African violets and gesneriads through her local botanical garden and got me interested again. I went to a local club meeting, started getting involved, and just got hooked."

Violet Affirmation

It is, Penny further indicated, "really easy to propagate African violets. I must have propagated thousands of plants, but it is still really thrilling each time to see those first little green 'mouse ears' peep out from the soil. And waiting for buds to open, especially of a new plant you've never grown before, can drive you crazy sometimes—it seems to take forever. But it is so exciting when the blooms open—they are so gorgeous. I find this 'circle of life' very life-affirming."

For Marge, too, "nothing says hope for the future like putting down a new leaf—propagation by plant tissue. For personal satisfaction, I take out the tray of leaves to see what has come up while I wasn't looking. Growing anything is good for the soul, but African violets in particular can be 'little healers.'"

To prove her point, Marge mentioned a cancer patient whose plants had been neglected by her absence. "They were leaning, they had developed problems from her not being there, as she sat depressed in the middle of the room." But, even so, she felt her spirits lift "because the neglected plants also were *blooming*."

Emotional uplift is also the theme of Marge's story of a mother who was lovingly moved to West Texas from her family home. She now enjoys an apartment "full of baker's racks, where African violets and other gesneriads flourish, though she had never grown them before. Her daughter says, 'Mom wakes up in a garden every morning.'"

Sometimes things don't go sideways and the center holds with a radiant grace.

Acknowledgments

I have been telling gardening stories for over fifteen years. I am deeply indebted to many editors for these prior opportunities, which I hope have honed me well for this book. "An editor doesn't just read," Susan Bell aptly observes in *The Artful Edit*; an editor "reads *well*, and reading well is a creative, powerful act."

I am especially grateful to Chris Corby, publisher and editor of *Texas Gardener*, who took a chance on me when launching me as a garden writer. And then his encouragement kept me at it for many years. It is an honor to serve as a contributing editor at his magazine.

I am also indebted to Connie Dufner and Mariana Greene, gardening editors at the *Dallas Morning News*, who entrusted assignments to me for five years. For seven years, there were rotating editors at the *Austin American-Statesman*, including Brenda Bell and Janet Wilson,

Kate's red spider lilies

who vetted my stories there. Gretchen Heber edited my work during my time with her on the Central Texas Horticulture Council. And at *Texas Gardener* and *Seeds* Michael Bracken lent a good hand, too.

I am grateful for the close consideration two readers gave my manuscript, particularly for their helpful nudges made in the most generous spirit of collegial collaboration. I count myself lucky, too, that Shannon Davies, director of Texas A&M University Press, believed that my project might potentially merit their and her own attention.

Sara Dunham at Pumpkin's Patch (http://myfavoritesheep.blogspot .com) kindly shared her photographs of bees pollinating buckwheat. Tony Roca helpfully provided a photograph of beehives on his land. Emily Neiman at Native American Seed graciously supplied a photograph of big blue stem. And the homeowner in Garland, who prefers to remain unnamed, offered her photograph of the front-yard cedar elm we tried to date.

Here, too, I remember Kate Frost, a valued colleague who long ago gifted me with her divided *Lycoris radiata.* These gorgeous red spider lilies flowered radiantly that subsequent autumn, then went dormant for years; yet rebloomed once more very shortly after Kate's death and have not been seen since. *Sic transit gloria mundi.*

Selected Recent Works Cited

Adler, Bill. *Outwitting Squirrels*. Chicago: Chicago Review Press, 2014.

Armitage, Allan. *Armitage's Manual of Annuals, Biennials, and Half-Hardy Perennials*. Portland: Timber Press, 2001.

Ashton, Richard. "Figs: A Texas Heritage." *Texas Gardener* 27 (March–April 2008): 36–39.

Baker, Jerry. *Jerry Baker's Bug Off!* Wixon, MI: American Master Products. 2005.

Berliocchi, Luigi. *The Orchid in Lore and Legend*. Portland: Timber Press, 2000.

Bonine, Paul. *Black Plants*. Portland: Timber Press, 2009.

Clebsch, Betsy. *The New Book of Salvias*. Portland: Timber Press, 2003.

Coulter, Lynn. *Gardening with Heirloom Seeds*. Chapel Hill: University of North Carolina Press, 2006.

Cregg, Bert M., and Robert Schutzki. "Weed Control and Organic Mulches Affect Physiology and Growth of Landscape Shrubs." *HortScience* 44 (5) August 2009: 1419–24.

Flores, Heather. *Food Not Lawns*. White River Junction, VT: Chelsea Green Publishing, 2006.

Galle, Fred. *Hollies*. Portland: Timber Press, 1997.

Gillman, Jeff. *The Truth about Garden Remedies*. Portland: Timber Press, 2008.

Grant, Greg. "What Do You Want on Your Tombstone?" *Texas Gardener* 27 (May–June 2008): 25–47.

Hansen, Eric. *Orchid Fever*. New York: Vintage: 2001.

Hanson, Thor. *The Triumph of Seeds*. New York: Basic Books, 2016.

Hart, Charles R., et al. *Toxic Plants of Texas*. College Station: Texas Cooperative Extension, 2003.

Hoblyn, Alison. *Green Flowers*. Portland: Timber Press, 2009.

Irish, Mary. *Perennials for the Southwest*. Portland: Timber Press, 2006.

Kenrick, Paul, and Paul Davis. *Fossil Plants*. Washington, DC: Smithsonian Books, 2004.

Köhlein, Fritz. *Iris*. Portland: Timber Press, 1987.

Lee, David. *Nature's Palette*. Chicago: University of Chicago Press, 2010.

Liggio, Joe, and Ann Orto Liggio. *Wild Orchids of Texas*. Austin: University of Texas Press, 1999.

Louv, Richard. *Last Child in the Woods*. Chapel Hill: Algonquin Books, 2008.

Mingo, Jack. *Bees Make the Best Pets*. San Francisco: Conari Press, 2013.

Nokes, Jill. *How to Grow Native Plants of Texas and the Southwest*. Austin: University of Texas Press, 2001.

Orlean, Susan. *The Orchid Thief*. New York: Ballantine Books, 2000.

Platt, Karen. *Black Magic and Purple Passion*. Sheffield, England: Black Tulip Publishing, 2004.

Pollan, Michael. *Second Nature*. New York: Grove Press, 2003.

Robbins, Paul. *Lawn People*. Philadelphia: Temple University Press, 2007.

Shoup, Michael. *Empress of the Garden*. College Station: Texas A&M University Press, 2013.

Silvertown, Jonathan. *Demons in Eden*. Chicago: University of Chicago Press, 2005.

Steinberg, Ted. *American Green*. New York: W. W. Norton, 2007.

Turner, Matt Warnock. *Remarkable Plants of Texas*. Austin: University of Texas Press, 2013.

Wasowski, Sally, and Andy Wasowski. *Native Texas Plants*. Boulder, CO: Taylor Trade Publishing, 2003.

Wasowski, Sally, and Andy Wasowski. *Requiem for a Lawnmower*. Boulder, CO: Taylor Trade Publishing, 2004.

White, Katharine. *Onward and Upward in the Garden*. New York: New York Review Books Classics, 2015.

Index

Page numbers in *italics* indicate illustrations.